The ^Messy Joys of Being Human

The Messy Joys of Being Human

A Guide to Risking Change and Becoming Happier

Helen Rosenau

Your Jewish Fairy Godmother

Riverview Press ≈

www.riverviewpressoregon.com

First Edition

Printed in the United States of America

Cover and book design by Vinnie Kinsella

Author photograph by Holly Andres

ISBN: 978-1-7325337-5-2

eBook ISBN: 978-1-7325337-0-7

For information about special discounts for bulk purchases or for information on booking the author for an event, please visit themessyjoys.com

For Lily, always home...

I have a certain knowing. Now I want sight.
  —RUMI

The changes we dread most may contain our salvation.
—BARBARA KINGSOLVER, SMALL WONDER

CONTENTS

An Invitation

This book is for people who are trying to get unstuck from patterns of behavior or belief that keep them from change. It's for folks who want to stimulate their intuition, so it can guide them, and who want to live richly while they follow a spiritual path. And it's for those who want to become kinder towards themselves and others. I hope you are among them.

Truth up front: I have no magic formula, step-by-step guide, or guarantee of anything except greater self-awareness. Believe me, if I had The Answer, I'd be shouting it out loud, along with the disclaimer that it might be total bull. Anything I have to offer comes from a lifetime of trying to make my own life happier and from decades of helping folks through life's tangles, as Helen and as Your Jewish Fairy Godmother.

What's here comes from changing—eagerly or after lots of stumbling and resistance—to become happier myself. It comes from every new beginning and every vow made and broken, and made and broken yet again a thousand times. It comes from books, teachers, friends, movies, and lots of quietude, plus many hints whispered and shouted from the world of the unseen. Some of that guidance I was smart enough to listen to. Some I accepted only after clunking my head repeatedly against my karmic homework.

Life is complicated. No one gets it right all the time. We're all trying to excel at some things while we survive so many others. We alternate between rampant pride at what we're best at, and uneasiness around what we're not. Mostly, our plates are full just getting through our days and years. Our stories are the unifying thread. They're how we define ourselves, how we explain ourselves to others, and how we organize our way of seeing the world and our place in it. In our time together we will unpack the old stories and create new ones to guide us to a better future.

This work is harder in the beginning. Once you engage you'll start to feel changes. Then you'll have more energy and excitement about the process. I'm asking you to use skills that might be rusty. They include honesty and self-reflection, and they'll guide you towards courage and curiosity. If you feel resistance, push even just a little more. You'll surprise yourself in the best of ways.

Before we tackle change, we'll look at our emotional innards. I'll share tools from my emotional and spiritual toolkit, drawn from traditions I've studied and practiced. I pull from a wide range of sources because I'm eclectic. Also, because what works for one situation may be useless in another, and what works in some phases of life may be inaccessible or stall out in a different cycle. Use what resonates for you.

We'll spend time in the messy middle and on the happier other side. We'll talk about what holds us back or pulls us forward, and what makes us feel brave or small. We'll look at our patterns of self-sabotage, searching for the sweet spots where happiness comes with less drama and pain. We'll need to visit places we buried deep, got burned by, or tried to leap over. I want us to clean out those dark and crumbly places, toss old baggage, and lighten our psyches. If your path is like mine, you'll appreciate your hard-won knowing more now than when you were hurting.

We'll wrestle with personal lessons: love, generosity, and caring, all mixed up with wanting, striving, and hurting. If it works, we'll find new direction and oomph. Then we'll look at our collective homework: how to make a sweeter, more peaceful world. Along the way we'll talk about heart and soul, what makes us cranky or sad, and how much we cherish gifts like friendship and chocolate.

First, we'll snuggle up by the fire with some tea or brandy and get to know one another. We'll share stories about who we've been, and dream up better ones about who we long to become. As we do this work together we'll learn to trust ourselves more, because the true and future us's are headed somewhere new. We'll remember how strong we really are, get good at things we haven't tried yet, and generally come away feeling lighter, clearer, and happier. That's my goal. It may show up differently in you.

I'm indifferent to the specifics of your beliefs and practices. I care only that you're committed to becoming a better person. Some people I love have very different spiritual languages from mine, but we all agree on the importance of compassion, acceptance, and trust. That's the bottom line here. If you're more focused on material things, there are better places to get a boost. This book is for the messy gardener. The one who appreciates invasive perennials and shaggy borders. For whom the joyous fecundity of nature is an invitation to get lost, wander, and play. It's for folks who see awe and wonder as a natural state, and want to find it again.

This book comes from everything I've integrated on my life journey. The author voice is a mix of Your Jewish Fairy Godmother Helen, the one who helps people move their lives forward, and just me Helen, down here in the weeds with everyone else, trying to get my messy life right. There are occasional touches of rabbi Godmother, mystical Helen (Kabbalah and more), the part of me who lusts for brownies, and the one who's happiest sitting with a book or my journal. Like Oregon weather, I move fluidly from one tone to the next, with this unifying thread: I care most that you and I and all of us become kinder, happier, and more peaceful together.

This book is my half of our conversation. I'll offer ruminations, insights, and questions. Your half is doing a lot of soul-searching. I ask only that you not abstain. Not be indifferent, hurried, or bored. If the words stop getting in, come back when they call you, when your answers ask to be born, and when your curiosity hungers for greater self-knowing.

Liking whom you see in the mirror is both a great beginning and a great goal. This work is not always easy. But even with uncomfortable, hard, or scary moments, I hope you'll become better at forgiving the pain of old wounds and at avoiding new ones. If you wrestle with this work, you'll discover new resources to make the life changes you want.

I'm making a map and hoping my karma road intersects with yours. In the universe of souls our connections are clear and bright. In our human-hood they can get tangled. Like the pilgrimage stories I used to love, we'll discover more on the journey than we can envision now. I can't promise enlightenment or even a cure for insomnia. But I'm betting these words can help speed you on your path and soften the rockiness along the way.

Deeply liking yourself is like first embracing your beloved after a long time of wanting, taking pleasure in the unveiling, until you're both a little more naked than you thought you'd be. But you're ready, and it feels good, and it opens so many doors.

Your biggest commitment is staying open: inviting knowing to thunk into place so you can move forward sure-footed and clear. Then we'll do it again. Because after the stuff, there's always more stuff.

I hope you'll join me. Take good care either way—

Helen

SECTION 1

GETTING TO KNOW US

*Vulnerability is the birthplace
of innovation, creativity, and change.*
—BRENÉ BROWN

This story has a happy ending.
—YANN MARTEL

In the Beginning

As I wrote, a friend reminded me about readers' love of authors' origin stories: folks who'd fled capitalism for a guru or discovered new forms of energy healing during life-changing upheavals. What about mine? Not as dramatic but more seasoned. Some of you already know me from my advice columns. To others I'm saying a first *Hello*. This section is a brief window into my life; more stories are woven throughout the book.

My perspective on change has been honed over time, like a diamond carefully being shaped. It's been a lifetime of living my story *du jour*, wrestling with my karmic homework, and searching for answers that made me feel more whole. It took me decades to make real progress, though it doesn't have to for you. My story includes long times of not knowing, wrong turns, bad choices, and staying stuck. There was no catastrophic moment. Instead, over months and years, my personal traps slowed and hurt me. Over the decades, they also taught me invaluable lessons.

I'm an energy junkie in the best of times, and a slacker in the worst. I'm thankful for every gift and blessing, but have been hungry for results I wasn't always willing to work for. Osho tells the story of a village woman who became enlightened at the sound of her chapatti dough touching hot oil: *Splat, pop, satori!* I cannot show you that road. I wish I could. All I can do is show you how I've learned, and hope your path will be shorter and easier.

My spirituality is layered and complex. I'm genetically Jewish, emotionally a pantheist, intellectually a Kabbalist, intuitively a Buddhist, and ultimately a mystic. I care about why we're here and about making the world and each/all of us better and more holy. I'm happiest seeing deer on my morning walk and feeling like the universe is talking to me. Sacred things are a core passion, but I'm also reflexively irreverent, and can get distracted by wine, women, and song. We've all got those seemingly irreconcilable parts, like conjoined Lily Tomlin and Steve Martin in *All of Me,* lurching along arguing about what to do next.

The bio's easy: I grew up in Philly, the eldest child of Jewish immigrants who fled Nazi Germany. LA in the '70s: grad school, coming out, drinking in wisdom from ancient practices and New Age arts. I've lived in Oregon since '81, semi-reclusive in my cottage and garden, doing my spiritual and emotional homework. My language and metaphors are a mishmash of this meandering path. I'm an inconsistent practitioner of anyone's forms including my own, but they're well earned and I rely on them.

The Dalai Lama, a hard guy to argue with, says it's best to learn from your own tradition. My return to Judaism came on my fifty-third birthday, walking through a bookstore and picking up a divination deck of the Hebrew alphabet. Around the same time, I launched my alter ego at yourjewishfairygodmother.com. I've always been the person people came to saying, *Please help*.... I offer motivation, inspiration, support, and problem-solving to clients and readers. But columns are brief, blunt advice about short-term problems. You can read a thousand examples on the website. A few hundred words cannot address the deeper and more complex issues we all face. Trying to wrap my arms around those struggles is why I wrote this book.

Chances to grow are rarely easy or fun. My heart and ego have been shredded more often than I like to remember. I stuck with relationships and jobs I should have left. I missed out on better ones because I felt unsure. Now I know more quickly when my choices ring true, and I've learned to trust that knowing. Along the way I learned that I could learn, which is no small thing in itself. I'll get as far as I can in this life, and then pass the baton to the next Helen, whoever she may be. I'm leaving her as many clues as I can.

As a counselor once wryly observed, I have a "rich inner life." I've asked myself Big Questions for decades. "Am I ready?" took up a lot of time, as did "Why me?," "Why now?," and "Do I really have to do this?" My hurdles have been real, not imaginary. I spent decades struggling to change my relationship with food and my body, to create healthy relationships, and to focus my restless intellect. Fortunately, I've always had good friends and spiritual curiosity. I rely on my deep connection with the world of the unseen, which is how I talk about God, gods, guides, totems, and other teachers we encounter, whether they're incarnate or ineffable.

If I advocate any practice, it would be this: Be still and quiet; then listen, listen, listen. If you have just one takeaway from the book, let it be that. You'll still need to act in ways that may require true grit, something you may fear you lack. Remember, it's not an easy jump, to go from Old You to New You. When giant steps happen they're a reward for the times of hard slogging. Keep reminding yourself that the shifts won't occur if you don't begin. Like the old joke about the man who cursed God because he never won the lottery, and is answered by a heavenly, "Did you buy a ticket?"

This I know for sure: If you sincerely move in the right direction, putting one foot in front of the other, something changes. You trust yourself more, and doubt so much less. You know what to do with less hassle or hand wringing. You like and love yourself in deep ways that help you reinvent yourself from the inside out. Whatever you call that, having more of it is what this book and my life are all about.

Playing Together, and Things
I Want to Know About You

The first title for this book was *The Book of Questions.* They're how I think we learn. We face tough ones in relationships, career, and choices of every flavor including time, money, food, politics, and how we treat those around us. Some answers we run towards. Others we dodge. We mostly want solutions without pain or hassle. Most of us are skilled at deflecting, at being defensive, analytical, sentimental, or just plain stubborn to avoid the gnarly truths that are staring straight at us.

Why? Because we're human. And that's a wonderful and messy thing to be. The joys are fabulous. And, as much as I hate to admit it, the non-joys are both good teachers and a marvelous source of more questions. Not just the *What the @#$%&!, Why me?, Why now?* kind we wail in crises. But also *How could something so wonderful have turned into such a massive pile of poop?* and *What do I do now?*

The questions I'll pose are meant to be evocative, not defining. I'll share answers I found on my own journey, and I won't ask you to go anywhere I have not. Always remember, your process gets top billing. If a memory or thought stream calls you, put the book down and pick up your pen or keyboard. I can't predict what will touch you or how. You'll hear the questions you need to. I hope you hear the answers too.

Making progress is all about listening for answers, or at least recognizing good clues. As you journal or share, don't be shy about revisiting parts of your life you might've walled off and hoped everyone else has forgotten too. Confession: I was the person in my sixth grade class picture with her eyes closed. I'm sure the photographer had several proofs to choose from, but he picked the one where I looked like a total dork. Worse, I was wearing the dress that just weeks later would split a seam at a family gathering, earning me taunts of "Helen's getting fat!" If only reality had delete buttons.

That kind of memory may seem small. But we all have those moments and worse tucked away: hurts that taught us to hide essential parts of ourselves, lest they become bruised again. It's time to unleash the grip those buried nasties have on how you relate to yourself and others.

One of my favorite mottos is "Take good notes." I believe in journaling and in shooting yourself an email whenever you have an insight, even at 2 a.m. From now until you close this book, whenever I say something is worth thinking about or pose questions (even if they aren't in italics), it's a *please-grab-your-journal-and-think-about-this* prompt. If this book is going to be useful, you'll need to do the work.

When the medics haul me off, they'll find a stack of illegible scribbles in my kitchen — insights that seemed urgent in the moment. If simple reminders like *Drink more water!* actually worked, imagine if you aimed higher, towards emotional and soul goals. I believe with all my heart that the big insights will keep knocking until you let them in. The sooner you acknowledge them, the more welcome they will feel, and the sooner you'll make more progress towards your goals.

According to sages far wiser than me, being human is a reasonably high state of being. Even if you believe in only one incarnation, it's time enough for so many complicated stories: love and happiness, sadness and grieving, laughter and adventure, curiosity and creativity, and a thousand small shames and blames that make the bad times harder and keep us from celebrating the good ones with joy and abandon. I'm always curious about other people's paths. Not just folks who look like they've got their shit together, but the ones I see wrestling with their stuff, as I do with mine. I want to hear their stories, learn about their struggles, and compare notes about what works and what doesn't, and about how foolish we feel when we keep repeating the same mistakes.

We're living in the golden age of story. Not just fiction, but social media, blogging, investigative journalism, public confessionals, and (sigh) even "fake news." It's an evolutionary shift that's changing how we communicate on a planetary level. So pay attention to all the stories: yours, mine, those I'll share, and those that surround us. They all shine a light on our transitions. You can do this work alone, in a dyad, or with a group. Consider yourself invited to post your stories and insights at themessyjoys.com. If your book club adopts this for a read, email me for a video call. If I ran the world, which sadly or luckily I do not, we'd create an active community of healing to propel us all forward.

If you're like the rest of us, your heart's been broken at least once, you've failed at things you'd hoped to do well, and you've been knocked around enough to know life's road isn't straight and flat. Mostly we think we know how we got to now. But when we tell our stories and tropes, we're more spins of the wheel since they happened or since we told them last. Our emotional innards have morphed, and, if we're evolving, our perspective has shifted. Now's the time to let truth visit with less need to embellish or obscure. To smile at an old friend without feeling any big *Yikes, not you again!*

I imagine us on a plane ride or a long walk, or learning one another the way people used to do, on a pilgrimage or as neighbors, sharing our before-I-met-you times. I'd ask you lots of questions and we would learn one another deeply.

I'd ask you:

Who are you?

What do you want your life to have more and less of?

What sparks you, makes you feel alive, creative, and juicy?

Who do you love, and who loves you?

How would your best friend and your worst nemesis describe you? Are any of those words the same?

What have been your biggest triumphs and worst failures?

What have your friends stopped trying to tell you, hoping you'll finally figure it out?

*What gives you drive and courage? What are you afraid
of in the wee hours?*

The point of this soul-searching is to get us closer to the
people we want to become. That may seem to happen at an
ungodly slow pace, but there are moments of grace, glimpses
of something more beneficent than we'd secretly feared. I
hope that together we'll accelerate growth, clear out the
underbrush, and make more room for joy, plus whatever
friends she brings along. Because the most important thing
I want to know about you is this:

Are you ready for change?

WHAT WE BELIEVE

I'll go first:

I believe in goodness, kindness, self-care, and boundaries—in all their tangled mating.

I believe we all deserve to be happy and safe.

I believe in sitting quietly and breathing slowly. I believe in meditation, but the daily discipline eludes me. Watching a fire in the hearth or the wind in my garden, I can let thoughts drift by without getting snagged by them. Then I wonder why I ever resist.

I believe in the healing power of art, whether I'm making or appreciating it. That includes images, words, music, movement, cooking, and any form of creativity you can conjure.

I believe in living with awareness and intention. I'm working on that.

I believe the universe is magnificent and vast, sweet and personal, a fabulous playground for the senses and the soul. In my naïveté, it looks like a grade-school picture of space-time winking *Hello*. I believe we can become our own higher selves, maybe even get to shout a hint or two through the veil, like in the movie *Interstellar*.

I believe in the lessons. Always the frigging lessons.

I believe it's never as easy as we wish it would be, and that we each get a different menu of chocolate and crap.

I believe in having an active personal relationship with whatever or whomever you believe animates creation, and being receptive to the world of the unseen. I believe listening is always the right answer, or the right way to find it.

I believe we're all just a nanosecond from remembering the answers we need to know, and that the universe tilts toward our best and highest good. If only we cooperated, the world would run more smoothly.

I believe in the power of words: to conjure feeling, create intention, forgive failure, and encourage us to try again.

I believe that most of us genuinely care about becoming better people, even if we regularly hurl invectives at lousy drivers or trip over our glorious imperfections.

I believe in acceptance and surrender, but I can procrastinate with the best. Rules almost instantly evoke my bristly teenager, and, no, that doesn't fade with age.

I believe in our ability to communicate, touch, and love in a manner so transcendent that we can heal together. I cherish meeting the ones we love so deeply we cannot imagine a world without them. And I hate the pain of loss, even knowing it comes for us all.

I resent the tyranny of time and of having to make choices in the same way I resent that kale isn't chocolate.

I love how I feel when I write, and how that sense of being hooked up ripples through me. I believe in regularly giving gratitude.

I believe that by wanting things hard and deeply enough, we can nudge the world in the right direction. And I believe that's not enough, that we need to follow up by doing our work.

And you?

What matters to you, beyond the lives and health of those you love?

What shapes your heart and your days?

How did you find and embrace those beliefs?

Are they flexible? Do they limit you?

How do they guide and inspire you?

What Do You Really Want?

We're each filled with so many micro-me's. The ones we've been, the ones we're becoming, and the ones we wish we were or hope others see us as. The "What do you really want?" question is for all of them.

It's a rare person who has nothing in their life they'd like to be different. Most folks answer with a litany of familiar wishes: to be thinner and healthier, have more money, a better job, a sweeter partner, all the adult versions of a shiny, new, red bicycle, or perhaps just "Win the lottery". That's assuming of course that they're safe from violence, have a reliable source of food and shelter, and a means to provide the same for those they love.

Almost all our desires implicitly require changes, and that's changes both in us and in the outer world. That likely means changing how we think about things and how we act. The old cliché about change is that it's usually motivated by a push or a pull. Sometimes it's easy: *I want him, her, or it now!!!* Whatever or whomever you're lusting after, anticipating, or even dreading to be over, you're like a weather vane in a hard wind. When I taught statistics, explaining binomial distributions was easy. In binomials there are only two options: *Yes/No, True/False*, or everyone's favorite: *When the phone rings, it's either your new true love or who-the-hell-cares.* Unless we're trying to beat a bad diagnosis, we're rarely as mono-focused as when we're falling in love.

Even when we're clear on what we want, most of us undermine our professed goals, if only by passivity or procrastination. We're skilled in the arts of self-sabotage: endlessly juggling pros and cons, old-fashioned stalling, and hours of worrying and tossing and turning in the wee hours, fretting about how things might go horribly wrong. Even our positive scenarios often have more emphasis on magical thinking than applied hard work. These old habits are well honed and are our go-to response patterns. Even when they don't work, we cling to them out of comfortable familiarity. I hope you're ready to leave these patterns in your past.

Fantasizing about clearing your path of obstacles (real, perceived, or feared) isn't all hot air and wasted time. It can reinforce your hopes and aspirations, although it's a rare person who doesn't want to get to goal quickly, without crisis or drama.

My favorite coaching tool is asking lots of questions and spinning *What if*s. Sometimes I start at clients' preferred outcomes, and then nudge them past their comfort zones. With others I go first for the wild edges, to see if I can expand their vision. Either way, I'm trying to help them figure out what they are, and are not, willing to do, say, and accept. This helps folks get clearer and more determined about starting the change process and understand that it's not just add water and stir. There are real decisions to be made and metaphorical dragons to face, both inner and outer.

Change is a messy process, but the twin joys of beginning and succeeding are fabulous, and the messy middle offers so many opportunities for self-knowing and becoming braver.

Your values and moral elasticity will determine what you'll do to manifest your desires. They're like the bumpers we give children when they learn bowling: they bounce us back to what's possible instead of letting us sail down the gutter. But for your imagined happiness to be more than a pipe dream it needs more than wanting.

We stay stuck for lots of reasons. Among the classics are believing in failure or lacking the oomph to begin. If you can crack those, even briefly, exploit your energy. Focus on small acts of regular accountability: a food log, reps at the gym, a weekly budget. They'll keep your go-for-it muscles tuned and ready for a sprint. Regularly chasing the little choices (one meal, workout, or paycheck at a time) will help you manage bigger challenges and help you see you're making progress.

But if your heart and soul haven't fully signed on for this ride, you're not going to get all the way to where you want to go. Something deeper needs to open and shift.

When I was younger and more ambitious, I did a visioning collage: a mix of worldly aspirations and seeker goals. I stumbled on it recently and saw *NY Times bestseller*. I laughed and had a surge of appreciation for that younger me. In 2003, after a burst of publicity for Your Jewish Fairy Godmother, I was flooded by requests for radio and TV appearances, by book agents, etc. At the same time I heard about an eBay pioneer, a guy who'd traded up in a mere dozen steps from owning a red paperclip to owning a house. He was barraged 24/7 by *tell-me-your-secret* calls. Ugh, no thanks. A friend says we each have to choose between The Big Life and The

Little Life. I didn't write a book then because my life felt out of integrity. In the years since, I've made many shifts and experienced lots of soul searching and spiritual testing. It's given me a deeper understanding of how hard we need to prepare before we earn and fully embrace results, even changes we deeply want. Without doing the deep prep work, wanting is like throwing seed on a field that hasn't been tilled or fertilized and expecting a great crop; it doesn't happen.

To me, being human is part of an ongoing conversation that's mirrored on the soul level. We're here in material reality while all around us, in some form of energetics science has not yet decoded, each of our small gazillion billion trillionth part of universal energy is interacting multi-dimensionally with all the other forms it can take (people/places/things, all that is/was/will be). In this vast sea of possibilities we're neither passive nor in charge, though we tend to learn that the hard way, after repeated bouts of stubborn will.

Trying to micromanage the world around you is usually a waste of time and energy. But that doesn't stop most of us from trying, and trying, and trying again. We'll do everything and anything to make the world around us more compliant. *Ha!* It's like the old joke about rearranging deck chairs on the *Titanic*. If we're smart or lucky, we learn a little with each try; the thumps and bruises crack open our too-hard places and give us access to deeper wisdom.

Both science and spirituality have concluded that our focus and attitude help shape what happens around us. See the movie *What the Bleep Do We Know!?* or read *The Hidden Messages in Water* if you want visuals. If you're consciously part of that conversation, the story leans towards you. If you're not, it can take lots longer. The key is living with awareness and intention. That can take lifetimes to master, but the teachers tell us it is completely accessible. It's like the slogan from *Friday Night Lights*: "Clear eyes, Full hearts, Can't lose."

Sometimes, if we're lucky, folks around us are paying off their own karmic dues in ways that shower us with chocolate instead of crap. But for most of us, our stories cycle through an oft-repeated script: *Hooray! Uh-oh...No, not again...Yikes! Help! Hit the reset button please.* Followed by a resurgence of hope. We keep going around and around until we crack the immediate problem or our consciousness shifts into a higher gear.

I'm talking about a shift in soul-level consciousness. The kind that, when the voice in your head asks, *If you had just one wish for this life, what would it be?,* you go deep, deep, deep, past ambition and pleasure, and don't waste your answer. That happened to me in the early '90s, at a pivotal point in my emotional life. I was in a bodywork session when I experienced a trance state. The voice felt deep inside me, but I knew it was not mine. It was a defining moment that would shape the direction and focus of my life. My answer was, "To live a life of goodness, joy, and creativity." Now I'd add a few, but that's still a helluva place to aim for. I hold it as my standard, even as I'm living it more each day. I also liken it to the sign in the auto repair shop: "You can have it fast, cheap, or right. Pick any two."

I sometimes joke that I'm the love child of Anne Lamott and Rumi. Why? Because she talks so eloquently about things I care about deeply, and is wise, funny, and unafraid in the telling. And Rumi because he's a mystic who calls God "The Beloved" and understands that being human is such a powerful blend of the holy and the visceral. Between them so many of my values are clearly and wisely spoken. Through some miracle of time, blessings, and hard work, I've gotten to a place where I'm generally happy when I wake up in the morning. When aging knees and random memory lapses seem a fair trade for a more solid, peaceful optimism—the kind that makes me more grateful, curious, and unafraid. That gives me energy rather than draining it, and that helps me manifest, in my simple way, what I most value.

Some of the growth happened because I held myself more accountable. We all push a little harder to win when we have a target. If you doubt me, buy a fitness tracker. And if you need a laugh with your motivation, Google David Sedaris's article "Stepping Out." For me, "winning" means moving from sweet spot to sweet spot with less wasted energy, time, or drama. And, yes, 10,000 steps a day whenever I can.

Despite our different packaging and problems, we're all pretty much on the same road. But we choose different paths to what we really want. Some will choose big lives and others smaller ones. The only wrong choice is staying stuck where you don't want to be.

Together we keep this world spinning, each choice impacting the whole. My grumpy day can make yours a lot worse; and your kind word might make mine better. Daily life regularly imposes quizzes to test how we're doing. Most of them boil down to immediate vs. delayed gratification, or stepping up where we might turn aside. How you answer these smaller tests keeps you healthy and happy. Or not. Because when bigger dramas take over most of us get sucked right in. Our aspirational, holy selves get sidelined for the one who needs to put out the fire and herd everything forward.

But if you don't also tend to your soul, it's like living in analog: you're missing big bandwidth that would make life easier, whether it's a big life or a little one.

Here's a journal entry from a long while ago. As a path I think it creates itself, and it's where I hope this journey takes us:

Live simply. Pray more. Stay healthy. Live quietly. Trust time. Let yourself find what you need to know. Even if you do not hear it in ways that you fully understand, the healing is happening. Calm your spirit. Seek beauty and blessings. Create ritual. Savor each moment.

Find ten minutes when you will not be interrupted.
Choose a quiet, comfy place and gently close your eyes.
Do a few breath cycles.

Then ask yourself: If I had one wish for my life, what
would if be?

Write down whatever shows up. No changes. No judg-
ment. Stay open for more flashes of insight because they
will come, but pay special attention to what showed up
first, both the words and any imagery that flashed in.

I want you to love yourself so much that you'll face
anything to become that you.

OUR MESSY JOYS

At the sound of love's flute, even the dead
tear apart their shrouds with desire
—RUMI

We walk through so many myths of each other and ourselves;
we are so thankful when someone sees us for who we are and
accepts us.
—NATALIE GOLDBERG

24/7/365

Life is a complicated process, even just the here and now, let alone the karmic threads we drag in with us. We have fabulous days and horrible ones. Times when we feel run over by trucks, others when we feel invulnerable and omniscient. No one escapes these ups and downs, and frankly, life can get boring if it's easy and predictable for too long, even if it's healthy and safe. I say that from the comfort of a dry home, not on the road escaping war, abuse, famine, or natural disaster. But for those of us with the luxury of introspection, it's worth looking at the hows and whys of our daily habits.

Most of our days fall in the murky middle. If you're lucky and blessed, you spend more of your time on happiness side of the line, with regular seasonings of joy and few of drama or tragedy. So what are all our messy joys? They're the parts of life we engage in with mixed emotions and even more mixed results; the choices and foibles that move us between a decent mood and a crappy one. The places where what you jump into completely and joyfully also causes disruption and sadness, to yourself or others. And the places that you enter tentatively that become your greatest teachers.

Some days, like ice cream cones, lean easily to the sweet. Other times, like after the end of a relationship, tilt hard towards sadness. Even if the hard times are mercifully brief, they can cause long-lasting impacts. Some things start off sounding fabulous and then turn to ashes. And oh so many fall into those places of complex emotions where how we act depends on our mood, the nuance and complexity of context, and on what story that we tell ourselves about what's going on at the time.

How we navigate these messy joys influences how we feel, the relationships we share, and the circumstances of our daily lives. As you read, note which feel familiar, in good ways or in painful ones. And as you work through the chapters that follow keep track of which situations and emotions show up most for you, and which ones trigger your coping behaviors, especially coping behaviors that feel like old, bad patterns. Having some wine or cookies while you process this material is a thoroughly reasonable choice if some of the words make you squirmy. We're aiming for happiness, not abstinence. We'll clean up the tough stuff soon and what you no longer need in your life will fall away as you become happier.

Each of the examples below can be a door to joy or angst, crisis and tragedy, or wonderful new possibilities. Don't rush as you read through them. If certain people, places, or events pop up more than once in your thoughts, make a note.

Dating, from high school to old age. Choosing between two romantic options. Unrequited love. Romantic relationships with a power imbalance. First kisses. Desire. Misinterpreting sexual cues. Affairs. Calling your partner by your ex's name. Ending a relationship.

Parenting.

Wanting people to like you. Trying to fit in. Secrets: held, shared, or busted wide open. Coming- of-age rituals. Meeting a great new friend. Losing an old friend. Knowing what you should do in a situation, but not wanting to.

Being an introvert or extrovert in the wrong place. Responding to "Hi! How are you?" when you have no idea who's asking.

Starting on a diet. Cheating on a diet. Ditto for your relationship with alcohol, drugs, gambling, or any other addiction. Learning moderation, patience, and discipline.

Judgments about others, coming in or going out. Self-judgment. Self-esteem.

Asking for what you want. Asking for help. Giving advice. White lies. Real lies. Putting your foot in your mouth. Apologizing. Forgiveness. Truth-telling.

Risk-taking, caution, and self-confidence. Public speaking. Performing solo at anything. Failing spectacularly. Learning a foreign language, a musical instrument, or new software. Technology in every form.

Family gatherings or class reunions. Changing your persona. Feeling like a kid, even when you're "old."

Physical dependence when you're ailing. Caring for a sick loved one.

Following your passions. Going all in no matter the consequences. Winning or losing something you worked hard for. Making decisions. Saying *Yes* or *No* before you're ready.

How do we cope with the feelings these situations evoke? We could dine on the good ones forever. For the not so happy, we respond with anger, frustration, jealousy, envy, and fear, as well as pain, denial, and withdrawal. Many of these situations imply that some changes are required, so there's also the subliminal (or active) fear that changing anything will mean more changes to come, so maybe we're better off living with what we know we can, even if we know it's not good for us or that it makes us unhappy. To some degree or another, we all practice those patterns, keeping big parts of ourselves hidden, a big loss for ourselves and the larger community.

We're not cowards or lazy; we're human. As every fairy tale, legend, Bible story, and millennia of tragedy and comedy attest, we often take the hard road. How much easier life would be if we were already the selves we wished to be. Note: This story doesn't end when you get to goal. With that comes the responsibility of being fully you out in the world. You need to step up to make not only your life better, but to make the world a better place.

As we wrestle with our messiness, we need to look at the roots of self-sabotage, at what makes us act out, lash out, and put up with behaviors that keep us stuck. That means visiting some tough emotional zones and doing what in elementary school we called "clean up, paint up, fix up week," making our neighborhoods free of litter and broken places. Only then can we think about change.

Think about the times and situations in your life when you've careened between bliss and despair or when good things turned sour. Is there a common thread or catalyst?

How do you act when things turn messy? Do you tend to damage yourself or lash out at others?

Are there patterns you have enacted so often you could write the script in your sleep? How do you feel during these dramas? How do you feel about yourself afterwards?

Do you try to keep your life in a narrow safety zone? That can limit deep funks but it also constrains happiness. Have you tried this way of living small as an emotional survival tool? How has it worked out for you?

Do you believe that your emotional and behavioral responses are inevitable, that you're somehow hardwired to fail in certain sectors of your life? Write down each of them, and take a moment to really feel where those feelings are rooted in you.

If you wrote a tweet with the hashtag #mymessyjoys, which would be your usual landing zones?

How about to #mymesssycopingmechanisms?

Light and Shadow

Holiness is a simple idea with radical implications: We've all got a holy spark in us, even if in oligarchs or angry exes it seems encased in concrete, or temporarily hidden when we encounter annoying people or long-stalled lines.

Namaste is the classic Hindu hello: "I greet the holy within you," delivered with a small bow towards the spark we're trying to recognize. Acknowledging at the outset that we're each a little pure makes the world feel friendlier; it's hopeful as well as polite. This attitude helps especially in stress-filled situations like "having a talk" about something serious, complicated, or emotionally volatile. Ditto for any kind of relating where we're more likely to meet the spark's opposite: the unhappy, unconscious, nasty, angry side of your partner, boss, friend, coworker, parent, child, nemesis, or random stranger.

We're all a little bit light. But we're also murky. I'm using "shadow" like a Jungian, not a racist, and, yes, I understand the power of language. Jews say *yetzer hatov* and *yetzer hara* to represent our tendencies towards better (*hatov*) and worse (*hara*) choices and actions. It's about direction and impacts, not about color.

I aspire to goodness, but my *yetzer hatov* isn't always in charge. Being happy often begets kindness. But when we're grumpy, it's a far bigger stretch. My *yetzer hara* is persistently devious as well as sulky and stubborn. I'm more likely to freeze up or hide than to challenge her. When our *yetzer hara* grabs the helm, the world gets less kind. The average bully or cheat is destructive in a narrow sphere, but any tyrant, polluter, or fanatic can impact humanity badly on a large scale. When you feel greedy for more than you need, look at why you're feeling pushy rather than shoving others out of your way.

Sadly, no one's shadow is invisible, benign, or endangered. When my besties are unhappy I can see all the ways they act out, and their squirming is no prettier than mine when I'm cranky or frustrated. Excessive piety, often wrapped in self-righteousness arrogance, is a traditional trick to hide one's *yetzer hara.* Easily spotted and hard to be around. Our least charming parts are especially vivid when we're judging others and telling them what to do or stop doing. That's doubly true when we're caught doing what we've criticized, though most of us take glee in seeing a nemesis' hypocrisy exposed.

When nothing in your life feels nourishing, it's harder to be nice to people, be they folks you like or those whose very existence pisses you off. Even when we aim for the proverbial light, our *yetzer hara* comes along for the ride. Unlike kindness' afterglow, your *yetzer hara* can make you snippy, snarly, and selfish. On any given day it may seem dormant, but it's as hungry as a shark, and very alive beneath the surface in most of us, easily triggered by big jolts or even seemingly small ones. The happier we get, the more quiescent it becomes, a win-win for us and all those with whom we interact.

Within a family, a *yetzer hara* that's perpetually nasty or abusive can damage others in ways that are hard to bounce back from. Living in that kind of unhappy context has complex implications, including training us to endure long periods of unhappiness. That can lead to the lands of repeated bad choices, which we use to endure and suppress our pain. Each bad path has its own long-lasting impacts. And then, because we're not totally unconscious, we feel doubly ashamed. We feel badly that we couldn't turn away the negativity that came towards us; and we feel badly that we're not taking better care of ourselves.

There really is bad energy in the world; it's not just in fairy tales or crime dramas. Sometimes evil intent is aimed at you, and other times it's just greedy to snare an unwary being. One night I Googled something that ended up terrifying me. The posting that got me curious should have been a warning. But I wasn't paying close enough attention: a good reminder about doing my blessings and prayers. After lots of muttering and lost sleep, I said, "Go away and don't come back!" Those unsought visitors did give me perspective, showing me that the darkest corners of my psyche are just a faintly dappled gray. I'm pretty that sure yours are too.

We're mostly holier than we fear. Lady Macbeth tried scrubbing murder off her hands. I'm betting your misdeeds or fantasies are far milder and less destructive. Truth is, our bad ain't really so bad. But even though I'd wish my bad urges gone, we're a package deal and we need to understand both our better and baser instincts.

Even on days we don't walk around feeling particularly holy, our *yetzer hatov* can show up. We help a friend, make a donation, volunteer time, or do some other good deed. Sometimes we get to play the hero, our *yetzer hatov* sustaining both us and those we love. But our subliminal ledger doesn't always register these acts of goodness. Far more often we're swimming emotionally upstream, fighting the tough feelings rooted in our *yetzer hara* that sap our energy and mood. What's in that toxic brew? A self-diminishing and often self-defeating mix of low self-esteem and low self-worth, plus pain, shame, guilt, and fear. Also the very wrong belief that we do not deserve to be happy. Talk about a recipe for sadness.

Where do these negative ideas come from? Usually from our childhood, be it from family of origin or another source. Bad stories we're told when young get in deep and have claws: a vicious pattern that's often reinforced as we grow. Each failure reinforces the last; our *yetzer hara* begins to organize how we see the world, ourselves in it, and how we respond to it. Eventually, with love, help, courage, luck, and sheer willingness to change our story, we can interrupt the cycle. But until then, our emotional baggage can become internalized so deeply that our own worst enemy might be living inside us.

Every family is organized around some story. In mine it was my mother's. She was nine in Germany when Hitler came to power. Powerful negative messages about Jews were broadly disseminated and reinforced by diminished civil rights, public shaming, and violence. There was no Jewish Lives Matter movement in 1930s Germany. As gifted as she might have been in a normal world, she lived her life tentatively, afraid to let her inner light show, lest it be hurt again by the *yetzer haras* of the world. Among the messages I learned growing up in a Holocaust family: *The world isn't always safe.*

In other families the story may be organized around alcoholism, sexual abuse, or violence, often shouted, beaten, and raped into the young and vulnerable. Some of the finest people I know were assaulted as children in ways that stagger the soul. For too long their inner light was dimmed by the evil acts of their perpetrators. Their insight, sensitivity, and willingness to confront abuse is a standard I wish no one ever needed to repeat. I don't think I have their courage. But it's a rare person who hasn't internalized guilt and shame that somehow we allowed bad things to be done to us, at any age, be those attacks passive aggressive, verbal, or worse.

Those tough feelings feed our *yetzer hara*. And no matter how wrong or ugly, messages about our low value get in. We sometimes believe we don't deserve a good life as much as other people do. A healthy, albeit long overdue, response surged in 2017 with the #metoo movement. But all the years spent holding ourselves back, settling for less than we deserve, is part of how the *yetzer hara* can diminish lives.

Then there's acting out. Instead of hiding, we make ourselves the center of drama. Sometimes we act out because we're cranky, bored, frustrated, angry, have low blood sugar, or are just being a jerk. But there's usually an underlying trigger. Our biggest off-track episodes can become life markers and stories, the kind of detours you keep secret, whisper about in the dark, or confess after a few too many. They're often dramas: making a noisy scene, having an affair, being wildly irresponsible with money, or even picking fights with the very people we rely on for emotional sustenance. You can count on apologies to be made when they're over, and hope the ones who love you are willing to forgive, and that their *yetzer hatov* is in charge when you need it to be. Your *yetzer hara* doesn't have much of a conscience. Your *yetzer hatov* should be kind to everyone.

At age seven, after losing a battle of wills with my first grade teacher, I stole candy from the local drug store, to the mortal chagrin of my mother. A decade later I acted out foolishly after what we'd now call date rape. Was I being evil? No. Was my *yetzer hara* running the show? Unequivocally. Did I feel guilty and ashamed? Absolutely. And did those feelings haunt and hobble me? Sadly yes, and for too long.

So how to get to higher consciousness instead of the land of rueful hindsight? Good optics in real time might help: spotting triggers before they start a chain reaction. But when we stub our emotional toes, our *yetzer hara* wants to feed on wine and chips, not on calm awareness. My balm is food. You have your own forms of self-soothing. But I suspect we share that moment of recognition after we've acted unconsciously, when we're holding a too-quickly-devoured bag of treats or hear the empty bottle clink into the recycling. That's when we wonder how we got there so quickly one more time, despite all our promises and hopes to do better.

An important skill in becoming our healed selves is remembering to choose the pause button in those moments, as in those moments before we act out. But learning to do that means being willing to wrestle with the old scarring and stories, not ignoring them or papering them over with immediate gratification, whatever your flavor of choice. To be very clear: just wishing away the causes and habits of unhappiness doesn't do squat. While I wish I could spare you, there's no jumping past process if you want change to stick. Sorry.

Maybe you can do this or on your own, or maybe you need trained support. But part of our being-here homework is noticing what tilts us one direction or the other, how we feel when we move that way, and how we feel after. Because each time you move away from your truest *What do you really want?* answer, it's like shoving your compass in a pocket and going off wherever the eff you please, without thinking about consequences or if you'll have any idea where the hell you are when your fit of pique is over. Eventually most of us turn ourselves around and remember what direction we were headed. But it can take a while, with lots of missteps and wasted time along the way.

Once you've taken steps back towards your real journey, make some time to see what triggered that particular bout of lust, greed, anger, or gluttony. *What was I running from?* is a good question to ask, because what you want to move towards is only half the story. Ask those hurt parts of you what they want or need, or if they're covering up yet something else that requires your emotional attention. It's all part of packing, and unpacking, your bags, for the journey ahead.

One note: Please, please, please distinguish between the stories that came at you, and the stories that you can and should make for yourself. Especially when you are feeling low, tell yourself the good stories: your sensitivity, your desire to heal, and your willingness to make the world a better place for yourself and others. Because those stories matter much more than the hard ones. We may never completely lose our old hurts. We can't negate the tough experiences of younger us's, but we can forgive ourselves for believing bad stories about us that were never true. We can treat ourselves better, and remind ourselves regularly that we are loved, valued, and on the road to happiness. And that we deserve to be.

Generally we think it's good to quell our less noble urges and encourage our better nature. But before you shove your *yetzer hara* under the rug, think about trying to walk around the lumpy middle. Avoidance and denial are short-run tactics, not healthy life strategies. Your shadow is here for a reason. Not so much to terrify or invalidate you, but to help you see what you're afraid of and to teach you how to tame that fear. Your homework is to face it, unpack it, and move forward lighter and freer. Yes, that sounds hard, but like water shriveling up the Wicked Witch of the West, once you apply light and love to the old, unhealthy stories, it's amazing how quickly your perspective will shift.

After you see what you've uncovered by this work, you'll see it mirrored all around: by a scene in a book or movie, friends you learn have a similar history, or seemingly random conversations landing on that topic. Synchronicity is your friend, so listen up. Pay attention not only to other people's experiences but to how they lived through and resolved them. Their stories may not fit you perfectly, but they'll shine a light that's worth looking at and offer another mirror for your process.

You need to be able to say, *Yeah, that's me*, and to name and claim it, whatever it your particular history is made of. Perhaps not on a first date or at a job interview, but clearly enough to remind yourself that we're all very much works in progress. Amazingly you may come to embrace your *yetzer hara* as a teacher. Perhaps not a kindly Yoda or Dumbledore mentor, but a deep teacher nonetheless.

Keep remembering that we're all powered by an inner light, connected by the Big Bang on the atomic level of stardust. That light is alive within you even when you're at your crankiest worst. It can suffuse you with peace, if you let it. You can never lose your holy spark, even if you stop listening to it for big chunks of time. It's the best of who you really are.

Don't reject your *yetzer hara* as worthless or bad. There was a great Facebook post that said, "Marvel at your life: at the grief that softened you, the heartache that wisen-ed you, and the suffering that strengthened you. Despite everything you still grow. Be proud of this."

What if you treated your shadow the same way? What could it teach you? What lessons do you think it has taught you already?

Remember times in your life—from childhood to last week—when you tilted far off course. Write them down, and let the list grow, as it will, over the next few days. That may be hard, but it feeds your healing, and that's why we're here. I promise they will hurt less and less as you do this work.

When you acted out, what were you really hungry for? What did you learn? Do you think you'd do things differently now?

What about your inner light? Do you remember to give yourself credit for your best parts on a regular basis, or do you only think about your flaws and failings?

Can you make space in your life to appreciate the good that you do and know that other people see it and value you?

Can you use a word or symbol to use as a mantra or trigger to remind yourself of your inner light? Choose one, or ask that the right prompt will appear. Then pay attention.

OUCH!

Buddhism teaches: "Humans suffer from the stories we tell ourselves." Those stories can engage us, comfort us, frighten us, motivate us, and keep us from change. They are worth unpacking and paying attention to, a process that can take lots of time and self-reflection. But when a heart or a back is aching, most of us reach for the quickest salve, even if that choice might hurt us more down the road. For real healing we need our heart, mind, and spirit in synch, lined up and aimed towards happiness. It's a rare being who can distill that magic brew in pain or a crisis.

We can't control how pain and suffering enter our lives. We can swear to avoid stupid decisions about whom to trust with our heart or assets. But sparkly love zaps and the lure of big bucks have seduced even the smartest among us. Short of a hermetically sealed room, we're all involved with other people for big chunks of our lives. We rely on them for everything from food and shelter to emotional nourishment. Even our dreams are attempts to wrestle with the unresolved and troublesome minutia of our days. And because people are complex critters, things get tangled, messy, and uncomfortable far faster and more often than anyone intends.

On the physical plane, these biological, chemical, mechanical structures we inhabit are subject to all manner of malfunction, breakdown, and decay. This doesn't just happen with aging. Scan the obits if you doubt me, or listen to your friends perform what a wise woman once called "organ recitals."

I had ear infections as a child, three or four times a year from six months old until corrective surgery in my teens. Each occasion followed a horribly painful script: a visit from the old doctor who served the German immigrant community with house calls. Imagine a man dressed like an undertaker carrying his black doctor bag. "Hello Frau Rosenau." "Hello Dr. Schless." After sticking his cold probe into my hot, throbbing ear, the ritual began: my mother held me firmly into the sofa cushions while he heated a long needle with a match until it glowed red hot for several inches. After warning me sternly not to move, he plunged it through my already inflamed eardrum. Imagine a volcano exploding inside your head. This is worse.

How did I feel? Hurt. Violated. Angry. Vulnerable. Self-pitying. Helpless. Rebellious. Secretive. Afraid. Mistrustful of authority. Determined to avoid any next time. In retrospect I see the experience as a form of abuse that more questioning parents or a better doctor might have spared me. But it's my story and it helped to shape me. The legacy of that pain impacted my physical and emotional future. I became an encapsulator, hoping to avoid trauma by masking symptoms until nature stepped in, and learning to hide my feelings, putting up walls, trying to blend in. Nice try. Life doesn't work that way.

If we can't avoid pain, can we control how we respond to it?

It's not easy, but you can try for dispassionate distancing, becoming a witness to your process, and trying to use reason to deconstruct what's happening. That assumes you can access your gray matter and it hasn't been hijacked by pain or rage. Understanding why we're suffering doesn't make it any easier or make what's hurting hurt any less. But it gives you something to grind, like the stick movie cowboys bite on while their buddy pulls out a bullet. After the drama subsides, you can see if self-knowing helps you suffer less. If not, next time work harder on considering possible consequences before you leap in a bad direction. But when you're in the throes of suffering, words can feel like a head game of Twister.

Pain is your body screaming for attention. A hand on the hot stove should teach you, though as the snarky quote says, "Experience teaches us that it doesn't."

I prefer my teachings without a lot of pain. In my Torah study days, I read about Abraham pleading with God before the destruction of Sodom and Gomorrah. If there were fifty righteous people could the city be spared? Forty? Thirty? Five? I felt such a sense of lineage. At heart I am a bargainer. I'll pay my dues when necessary, but that's theory not reality. I've inherited my father's disobedience around physical therapy and his reflexive avoidance of inflicting pain on myself. So my new knee reflects my eighty-percent commitment to health and deference to my aching quads. Sadly, those signs at the gym that proclaim "No Pain, No Gain" hold more truth than I'd like.

At age six, I was hospitalized for inflamed tonsils. In the adjoining bed was a head-banger: a kid who, for whatever source of inner pain, knocked his head against the wall re-peatedly (and thank God mostly in rhythm) until he was sedated or collapsed. I was young, and too into my own story to engage very much with his. But he stayed in my iconography as a shining example of how badly we can hurt ourselves when we're suffering.

There's the pain aspirin can quell, and the kind you fear even another few incarnations might not touch. Falling off your bike hurts. Ditto missing out on something you really wanted, like a prom date or promotion. Getting dumped can cause a literal aching heart, a pain I hope you've felt only rarely. Adults may rue, but can understand, pains like tooth-aches or pain-in-the-butt colleagues who ask questions in a meeting overdue to end. There's sharp, fast pain and the kind that festers long after the original injury. I imagine the head banger had both, likely without access to the nurturing that might have provided refuge and taught him that the world has softer places too, places where you can cry about what hurts, where someone might hold you and say, "Sweetheart, I'm so sorry."

We all deserve that kind of comfort. Many of us seek it for too long without landing in the arms of caring friends, partners, therapists, or other allies. We all deserve better. If you've made it to now, you're almost certainly carrying both too tender places and scars. If not, I'd love to meet you and I'm happy for your fortunate life. The trick is figuring out how to avoid more of them, and stopping them from hurting you more.

I once had a herniated disk. Stepping out of bed the first morning I thought I'd puke from the pain. The time between then and surgery gave me empathy for folks who live with chronic pain. A few years later, in my post–new-knee oxy haze, I felt a different sympathy, for the folks who hurt so much they'll blot out all feelings, the good along with bad. Headbangers of a different god, on a road to sad oblivion.

If asked on any non-achy day, I'd choose an injured body over a hurting heart. But on an everything-hurts-what-did-I-do day I'll deny having said that. Emotional wounds can hurt us just as profoundly. I've known incredibly successful people who suffered horribly as children. Even after they're grown and seemingly healed, there's still a small hole in the heart, a cloistered and tentative place, where they wonder if everything they've done and become is enough. We see the healthy outer, but they're holding that hurt little one inside, trying to smile or perform for us while they soothe or numb her.

We all have responsibilities for helping our close ones heal, whether it's support during chemo or listening to the wailing of your friend who's just been dumped. Their laments usually distill down to: *Why me?*, *How could I not have seen this coming?*, and *Please make it stop. I promise I'll be good.* Eventually what emerges is pale and weak; after the fever of suffering breaks, pain is no longer the compelling arc of their narrative. But it can feel like a very long time if you're the friend bearing witness and trying to put all the broken pieces into some functioning semblance of whole.

One huge problem is internalized blame. The very scary and almost-always-wrong idea that somehow you did something to deserve being hurt. That you're not *X*, *Y*, or *Z* enough, where your *X*, *Y*, or *Z* and mine might be vastly different, but each is a place we'll always be uniquely vulnerable. Mean people everywhere sense these wounds like a shark smells blood. Our most tender places are easy to sight when we're hurting, even if we try to act falsely secure and confident. And then, when we feel content and safe enough to let down our protective guard, some folks can see in deeper than we might be ready to allow.

Because we are intuitively self-protective we can become defensive, putting up emotional or verbal walls. We become prickly, passive aggressive, even cold and nasty, fearing what will happen if someone gets too close. Your way of masking or unloading your emotions might be very different from your best buddy's. Almost never, however, do the ways we protect ourselves with walls help our emotional development or healing. Often they become bad patterns that we use, consciously or not, to keep ourselves isolated, which in turn brings more patterns of bad behavior, including substance abuse and fear of intimacy. It becomes an unhappy cycle that's hard to escape.

Nothing beats fear for negative impacts. Fear may be intangible but it is all enveloping. It reinforces the idea that happiness will never come. Fear's a poison that negates anticipation and delight: a soul-killing virus that keeps you scared of being disappointed, hurt, or misunderstood. Fear can make you hold back from being open and risking vulnerability. Fear preempts the possibility of joy.

Every fear, scary thought, and bit of anxiety and foreboding you've ever had, stretched end to end, would probably get you to Neptune and back. Maybe more than once. All those neurons racing through your systems are carrying not just your now, but your history. No wonder being hurt again feels like crap. (So hard and so heavy to keep carrying: surely it's time now for some sugar or a nap.) But being fully alive means risking pain. If you deny yourself that, pain wins. And one thing I can promise you: there will come a time, a throw-the-dough-in-hot-oil moment of emotional enlightenment when you take your finger off the hot stove of pain and you say, *No more. Not that way. Not any more. I am ready to stop hurting.*

This may not happen quickly. There may always be scared or cautious places in your psyche. But over time they'll stop distracting you. You'll be able to look in that direction and find energy for change. You'll trust yourself to do better. Why? Because you're readier to become the healed you whom you so deeply aspire to become.

But sadly change is not one big decision followed by a great leap forward. Please don't shoot the messenger, because next we're going to visit the tender places of earlier us's. Not all at once, and we'll come bringing empathy and balm. It may feel like the least fun part of this book, but after fear of being hurt stops deterring you, you'll see your old wounded parts are just temporarily broken. They'll respond like kids to birthday cake when you reclaim and reinvigorate them. If you need motivation, remember you owe them a karmic IOU: They helped create this now you, the one who's primed to become happier. So go deep not light with this. As Dan Savage says so simply and eloquently, "It gets better."

How have you been hurt? Please think about emotional and physical wounds, from childhood to now. Each one has left an imprint, and not all those have been negative. But you need to be willing to look at them.

Do those places still feel tender? What kinds of situations or conversations bring up those memories?

How do you feel when that happens?

How does that impact how you relate to yourself or others in the moment? After?

How has your history of pain impacted your life choices big and small?

NOBODY HOME

A dolescents are easy to embarrass. When I was in high school, my father would answer the phone with a booming, "Nobody home!" Any boy too flummoxed to reply was not welcome in our gene pool. Then I wanted to strangle him; now I love the memory. We like to think we're inscrutable. But we're often far less so than we hope. Once you get past our online dating profile variations of sizes, shapes, colors, hobbies, and kinks, we're pretty similar in our hopes and fears. And most days pretty easy to read. Even trying to hide, we're as transparent as my father's joke.

Seeing in is easy for those who know us well, especially so when we're thrashing about in love or despair, or trying to make a big decision. What might feel to us like swimming through taffy is clear and obvious to our friends, and maybe even to perfect strangers, though folks we don't know well are usually more polite than our besties with their suggestions about what we should do or say. Whether we ask or not, we'll know what our buddies think because they'll tell us. And often tell us again and again: "You know I'm right! Just listen to me..."

I sometimes float a problem as though it's a Fairy Godmother column topic. This lets me watch how folks respond. I can gauge their insights and empathy without my own emotional viscera being too vulnerable. Someone once observed you can tell a lot about a person by how they treat stray dogs and shopping carts. That sets the bar pretty low. I care more about how they deal with sorrow or pain, and how they celebrate a friend's achievements even if they're in a bad place themselves. Sincerity and empathy mean more than words. But it's lots easier to solve other folks' problems than our own.

As a fiftieth birthday present, I installed a river rock streambed, with running water available on a switch. I added a suggestive sprinkling of black rock to move the eye and create a sense of momentum. But it's a trick. With feelings there's no easy con. You're either willing to ante up or you're not. Period. Remember the three monkeys with eyes, mouth, or ears covered? A classic way to approach the issues we prefer not to: the ones we consistently avoid facing, get a little queasy over, and feel vulnerable when we get too close to. You're either ready to be present with what's happening or you kick the problem into your future.

By the time we reach adulthood, most of us have gotten pretty good at this drill. With lots of practice we've become adept at deflection. We can slide a conversation sideways without even a blink. When we're droning on about our honey, our money, or our addictions, seeking sympathy but clearly not ready to change, a friend might try some tough love. There's an off-chance we'll soften, but mostly we ward off with, "I don't want to talk about that." End of discussion. A defensible perimeter most folks will respect until it's time for a bigger intervention. Usually life ups the ante and our friends help us through the next crisis or three. But unresolved emotions are an unsteady foundation on which to build a life. The more you try, the likelier a crash will occur. Maybe not today, but almost inevitably. It may come in a form unrelated to the original injury, but suppression is a set-up for future harm.

My brother, quite the wit, once said, "De Nile ain't just a river in India," to uber-emphasize the quote "Denial's not just a river in Egypt." That river runs deep and hard through each of us. A favorite story: A linguistics professor positing that many languages use double negatives for a positive, but none has a double positive for a negative, is answered from the back of the room, with a dry "Yeah, yeah..."

That's how strong denial's current is. Even while, in all your pious, healthy glory, you're fasting, juicing, icing, gyming, and sugar-, gluten-, and carb-freeing your way to health, if we are the same species, you're also stashing pints of Ben and Jerry's or bags of Oreos, plus scanning the calendar for birthdays, holidays, weddings, and other upcoming excuses for treats. If I had a dollar for every Monday I'd promised to "start being good" or "living on program," we'd both be rich. Reason, by the way, has very little to do with this process, so trying to quell avoidance and addiction with logic or high-minded principles is a losing battle, at least for me and almost everyone I know.

Most of us cover our fragile places by acting in ways that range from silly to outright self-destructive. Even when well-meaning folks we love and trust try talk to us about finding help or changing bad habits we act like three-year olds, plugging our ears and chanting, "I can't hear you, I can't hear you, I can't hear you."

Yeah, yeah...

Our avoidance behaviors can get quite elaborate. It's like the wondrous alt-worlds in movies like *Avatar* or *Mad Max*: intricate, compelling, and worthy of attention. Excessive eating, drinking, smoking, sexing, shopping, and drugging are quick trips to the land of denial. Each has its own short-run joys and long-run costs. But none of them solve our underlying issues. By the way, if you have ideas for different or seemingly better forms of distraction please send them ASAP, preferably with a coupon for a massage and a side of dark chocolate.

Denial's easy. Because microwave popcorn or brownies (death to their inventors) are just two minutes away, and everything exists on Google in just a few keystrokes and nanoseconds. Big things like love and success take a lot longer and are a lot tougher. But we've grown impatient, and our coping addictions are robust, well established, and ever so close at hand to comfort us. Sure they can. *Not.*

What's impressive is how skillfully we skate past contradictions between what we say we want and how we behave. We've been doing this dance so long we can do it in our sleep. And, ahem, doing it is what keeps us asleep, as in unconscious, even while we profess our desire for healing and transformation. It's like hand puppets boxing in the mirror: they keep whacking and whacking and whacking one another and no one wins.

In *The Americans*, a lonely FBI secretary is seduced by a charming spy. You keep shouting at the screen, "C'mon Martha, don't fall for it!" in somewhat the same tone that your doctor, mother, friends, and therapist want to say, "Stop! You know this is wrong. Just shut up and do what you need to!" They might all be shouting at top volume, but if you're rowing down De Nile you won't hear anything but the siren song of escape.

Until we're ready, we're pretty much primed for denial. Even on the river of change, we're most of us slow rowers, new at facing our crap, and easily distracted from rash vows of *Never again, I promise*. Not that anyone wishes you a slow trip to goal. Not you specifically. But like that fabulous German word *schadenfreude* (taking secret joy in the struggles of others), we like knowing there are other folks rowing hard nearby. Folks to complain to, who hear our earnest *I'm going to get it right this time, I swear!* And to commiserate with its good buddy, *#*&@!! I screwed up again*! We like knowing there are other folks fighting their own on-again/off-again battles. Not that you don't wish them well. But perhaps not so much well that they succeed a lot before you. Anne Lamott has a fabulous riff on this in her phenomenal book *Bird By Bird*. She tells stories of friends who won prestigious prizes, contracts, and awards before she'd hit her current stature, and gives hilarious examples of jealousy, all variations I mentally filed under *I should feel like a piece of poop for feeling this way*.

I'd tell you to join a support group, take vows, pay penalties, or impose any form of positive or negative reinforcement you can conjure, if I genuinely believed that anyone actually changes even a nanosecond before they're ready. But personal experience, decades of observing others, and letters from Fairy Godmother readers attest it's as rare as three full moons in a month. And while I'm all for trying to change every time you're motivated, without the prep work it's like putting un-risen dough into the oven. You get a hard, unsatisfying lump, and might start believing there's no point in trying.

Here's the good news and the bad: Life's a long run game and you are always "it." You and your denial are as tied as Sidney Poitier and Tony Curtis in *The Defiant Ones*, black and white inmates who escape a work-gang still chained together. They're "free" but trapped with their all prejudices and misconceptions. You're chained to your denial in a way that blunt force cannot undo. And you'll keep paying the price of that servitude until you're ready to be really free.

The costs of bad choices may be small in the short run, a headache or an overdrawn check to start. But when your doctor says diabetes or your accountant starts talking bankruptcy, you'll know the bill's come due. I'm betting hard you're not going to be any happier than the rest of us who've been there.

Imagine someone saying, "Tomorrow you're going to stop _____ing." [Fill in the blank with your favorite denial pattern.] What's the first thing you want to run and do?

Make a timeline of your life. When has _____ been a problem?

What triggers an eruption? How does it manifest? How long does it last?

When and how have you tried to change your relationship with _____? What motivated you to try? How long did you sustain a new path? What derailed you?

What's worked? What stops you from continuing to push forward or trying again?

RUSSIAN DOLLS

In mid-winter there's a Jewish holiday called *Tu B'Shevat*. In mystical terms it's *when the sap remembers to begin to rise*. Lovely. It's celebrated by ritual gatherings around plates of fruits and nuts. The assembled folks talk about what are called "the three kinds," which represent ways that we protect ourselves and how we interact with the world. The first kind includes things that are hard on the outside with their sweetness concealed (think almonds or oranges). It represents our outer boundaries, ways we protect our most intimate selves and hide in the illusion of safety. The second kind (say a peach or date) is sweet and inviting, but has a pit in the center. They represent our inner walls, the parts others might bump into if they come in too close. The third kind (like berries and grapes) you can eat the whole of. They represent us feeling joyous, living with a trust that doesn't require layers of protection. How you feel when you feel safe and happy enough to let your fullest self be seen.

Most of us vary our self-protective styles depending on who we're with, what our role is, and what local values and norms might be. In new love we might be one kind or in long-term family or work relationships another. Sometimes social personae can be a mask that serves us, helping us get through the day and protecting what's precious. I'm a right-brained mystic who worked for decades with left-brained materialists. On any given day if we'd interacted you'd have seen a smart, articulate rationalist, but that was how I learned to pass. I protected my true nature to do my job and pay the mortgage. I've done the same in conversations with people who are overly judgmental, though with age I'm winnowing my world more to those who make me feel more open and happier. Life's too short.

Some of your hurts are so old you might not remember their origin, though they've helped to form and shape you. When yesterday's insult lands atop your first breakup, teen-aged acne, or muffed chance to win the game, you feel it acutely. We've all had practice with that kind of hurting. Through trial and error, friends made and kept (or assessed and found wanting), we've learned where it's safe—and not—to share our emotions and wounded parts.

One excellent thing about being human is that we're fast learners. When we find a trick that works we practice it, even if the skill means being better at avoiding karmic homework than facing and resolving it. Because we prefer walking around happy rather than scared or sullied, we've learned to shove the emotionally threatening stories of our lives down deep, into our hardest inner kernel, behind the locked door of our heart, a place that holds every hurt or slight, all our guilt, shame, unmet expectations, and failures. Brené Brown has a picture of the protected heart as an armored locket, solid as a fortress. But that's a defense, not a cure. Scarring protects like a coat of shellac: it wears thinner with time. When we're bruised again, we keep shoving down what hurts, all the while deluding ourselves that this vault shouldn't interfere too much with how we live. Except of course it does.

To be 100% clear, when I talk about vulnerabilities, I'm not talking about experiences that make us more open and caring, and that teach empathy and compassion. Rather, I'm talking about the ones that carry sadness, shame, and distancing from our feelings in their wake. The tender places buried beneath bad decisions, addictive behaviors, and other escapist patterns. The ones we do everything to hush up and stuff down. The parts we would wish away if we could, and hide when we cannot. Those are the ones that make most of us armor up.

One of my favorite scenes in Ursula Hegi's brilliant novel *Stones From the River* (set in small-town, World War II Germany) is when her dwarf protagonist, who's secretly hiding Jews, is brought in by the Gestapo for questioning. The interrogator is repelled and fascinated by her and asks what life as a dwarf is like. She asks him to imagine how it would feel to have his worst secret pinned to the outside of his chest, like a beating heart, for everyone to see, today and every day, and to have to live with that acute vulnerability. That's what I think we fear when we think about others fully seeing us, the real and full us, in all our flawed and fragile beauty.

How we hide those parts of ourselves, the ones that we can conceal, is by constructing an elaborate emotional infrastructure not unlike nested Russian dolls—the kind in painted costumes, with a generational deconstruction as you open them: from the outer great-great-greats to the teeny baby, no bigger than your fingertip. They wear identical smiles, a painted-on veneer of politeness that might hide anything from bland forbearance to raw pain. They are as carefully assembled as we each morning, heading into the world, doing our work and playing our parts.

Those dolls represent how we've learned to protect ourselves. Each inner layer a more fragile and hidden you, all the way back to a you that you cannot even remember. A you who learned early that the world isn't always safe, and that it's better to hide what should not be hurt again. The heart of our work together will be your willingness to unpack the very places that you've spent much of your life avoiding, even as you've been adding to them like a miser with his hoard.

True healing requires going through all the hidden layers. Through the swallowed tears and false bravado. Everything you shied way from, slid sideways on, or went into full denial about. It's not all shame and guilt. It can be the smaller things, the times you were told to "just mouth the words," or overheard people talking badly about you. The sad, lonely, hard times of your life, when you were rejected, dismissed, beaten, and felt insecure, lonely, unwanted, beaten, and afraid.

Sometimes there are secrets you cannot share. When your child confides her fears or anguish. When a friend says, "You're the only one I can tell," or, "It's bad, but maybe the chemo…," while her voice says her timeline is already shrinking. As hard as it may be, you have to put those terrible knowings somewhere deep inside you to be able to comfort and be supportive, so you're not burdening your loved ones with your sorrow while they fight their battles. We have those compassionate little dolls too, as well as the hurting ones. But none of them are easy to carry, and that can sap the very energy we need most. Feeling helpless to wave my godmother wand and fix the world for the ones I love is among my least favorite feelings.

Sometimes our emotional proprioception simply toggles off—fast, hard, and securely shut down. One piece of bad news too many and suddenly it's nothing in, nothing out. Your teflon heart, well trained to shield, says, *Feeling's too damn hard so I'm not going to. Not going there ever again, no one can make me so stop trying.* Here's the hard truth: doing this work it is not easy. Visiting the hurting places may be scary and make you cry. Remember how wonderfully tears can heal, even for those who cry more easily at *Bambi Meets Godzilla* than after the end of a relationship.

I remember my mother in multitasking motion keeping her personal demons at bay: cooking dinner, baking, sweeping, and talking on the phone while she did dishes and aimed us towards our homework. But her brisk efficiency was punctuated by months of crying jags until she found a regimen of lithium to level her. The household became organized around *Don't do anything to upset your mother.* We each held a book, as a window to outer worlds and a wall to inner ones. Feelings were kept hidden lest they topple our calm. No wonder I felt safer stuffing emotions where they wouldn't disrupt the flow of life, a pattern it took too long to unwind.

The more we stay layered up, the more we stay reactive. Instead of healing, our hardnesses bump into one another. We knock each other off balance, intentionally or not. That might sometimes peel away a little paint, making a crack in an outer façade. But those cracks allow light and insights in. And get us re-connected to the world, if we let them.

In mystical Judaism there's a concept of *klipot*, layers that cover your inner light, that divine spark we'd all see in one another if it weren't hidden beneath old scars, the blacks and blues, armoring, and the pretty paint of the day. I imagine a hurricane lamp: our holy beings struggling to see out through the soot and detritus of life. If we could clear even a pinhole's worth of light, we'd see so very much better and more of our holiness could emerge. Even the smallest pinhole takes work. It takes courage to face our pain, old or new. Trust to look into the dark and believe there is a better beyond. Curiosity about one's own history, faith that healing is possible, and willingness to embracing the idea that we are worthy of the happiness we hope will follow.

We often struggle before we open the hidden places. Ditto when we answer tough questions with overly glib or familiar answers, a pattern that's distracting and counter-productive. It makes us avoid hard conversations because we think our answers are impervious to change. We're sort of right, because the answers won't change until we do. That cocoon of false knowing insulates us. It can become overly confining. It's easy to feel lost or trapped, and to want to run almost anywhere to escape confusion and scary feelings.

One way or another, your job is to peel back the layers until you find that littlest doll. You might hit big resistance, or discover that the wall you fear is really only made of tissue. Ironically, if it starts out feeling hard, you're probably on the right path. And the universe, bless her heart, will spill you into a ditch if you get cocky or lazy. And then you'll get to do it again, and again, and again after that.

There's no telling how long this work will take, but it is a big and necessary part of your journey. Eventually, the healing will come. Despite your fears and doubts and evasions. Beyond doubt and denial and all your worst tendencies, if you begin to do this work, you'll get closer to where you want to be.

Think of yourself as a beautiful Renaissance painting, obscured by the grime of time and yellowing varnish. What would it take for you to restore yourself?

What do you fear would happen if all your inner dolls peeled back their masks and the more fragile, tender you was revealed?

Write everything you fear people knowing about you. List your worst and most embarrassing secrets, even the ones you've never shared. Then take the paper and tear it into pieces. Burn them and throw the ashes in a river (or flush them away). It's calming (once you get past scary).

If you're not ready now, try this when your inner voice says you are. You will be, because these stories are knocking to get out. And you'll feel so much lighter once they're freed.

Repeat this exercise whenever you have demons that come to visit, be they new or old. Treat the process like a ritual and respect that it really has power. You are deciding what parts of your history to keep, and to which you can say Good-bye. Once you get good at doing this you will find new joy and strength.

NORTH STAR

In the millennia before the invention of GPS, sailors navigated by a rare fixed point in the sky: Polaris, the North Star. They found their way in open seas by trigonometry, invented by ancient mariners to measure relationships between themselves and the stars. It was elegant and reliable (once you knew how), giving some certitude in a world where all around was ominous, choppy, and dark; if a stormy sea didn't get you, sea monsters might. But, with luck, Polaris would guide you where you wanted to go.

Every vessel needs someone to keep the ship on course, towards a goal that may be very far away, which is how goals often feel, especially in big life transitions. Though we're sometimes unsure who should be at the helm, we want her/him to be trustworthy and steady. But yikes, on this vessel the default is us.

Medieval Germans created *narreneshiffe,* "ships of fools." Floating collections of exiles: the disabled, deformed, non-conforming, and seen-as-nutty-or-dangerous to others or the status quo. They were sent down the river. *Bye-bye. Go away. Don't come back.* Not In My Backyard in its original form. The river was their pilot and often their grave, as the currents took them from one inhospitable port to another.

Katherine Anne Porter's 1962 novel *The Ship of Fools* is about refugees on a ship fleeing Nazi Germany. My paternal grandparents were on such a boat, a mere two hours into Brazilian waters when World War II was declared. That's how thin the line could be between a new life and being shipped back to the ovens of Europe. It's a scene we see mirrored around us now far too often.

Sometimes—usually after a big karmic clunk on the head—we become afraid that our ship of self is being steered by our desperate, strange, and unwanted parts. In hard times we forget our strengths too quickly, even very useful traits like staying calm in a crisis or willingness to speak truth to power. When we see only our insecure, inept, and cowering parts, our *yetzer hara* (our negative energy) has won.

We're trained not to show our hurting places or anxieties, unless we're among our besties. Some folks use bravado; others, like Chandler on *Friends,* deflect with humor; and others burrow in deep and are seen as very shy. With practice and time we develop emotional perimeters we can feel safe within. But going shields-up takes lots of energy, which can distract us from making emotional and spiritual progress.

Imagine all your scariest parts packed together in a trunk that's straining to split open, like something in a Harry Potter novel. These parts are not innate. They're created by life experience, by the opinions of others and their projections onto us, views that we sometimes lack the self-confidence to reject. We take them in, and then muffle them to help us make our way in the world.

I recall attending a cousin's Bat Mitzvah at age nine. As the band started up, my mother said, "We don't dance," a crippling, joy-crushing sentence that took too long to toss overboard. Years later I took a movement class; each session started with meditation. A month in, before I knew what the image represented, I saw an elephant sitting on a throne, smiling at me and saying, "Get up and tap dance." I described it to my teacher, wryly observing, "Of course the klutz sees an elephant." She then introduced me to the Hindu god Ganesh, also known as The Lord of Attainment and The Remover of Obstacles. Would that all our healings were so vividly clear.

In every sector of our lives, body to mind, creativity to sports, many of us were given negative messages: *You're stupid. You're fat. You're a klutz. Girls can't do math. Please don't sing. You can't draw. Don't raise your hand so often. Stop showing off. You can't control yourself around food, money, sex, etc. No one will ever love you if you aren't more, less, or different.* And on and on. Implicitly, *Stop being so you!* Intentionally or not, these messages make us diminish ourselves. They turn into looping inner scripts, mumbled in our subliminal consciousness. Instead of courage and curiosity, we curl in and make ourselves a smaller target. Instead of being brave, we leave a smaller footprint in the world. I love the quote, "Success is going from failure to failure without loss of enthusiasm." Because each try makes us smarter and more committed.

Many of my inner scripts came from my parents, both of whom escaped Nazi Germany before World War II. They internalized many negative lessons from their youth, and they passed them on to us, by role-modeling, by epigenisis, and by not teaching us healthier counterparts that might have offered more strength and perspective. Here's a sampler of what helped form my childhood views of the world: *It's better not to be noticed. Bad things happen when people don't like you.* As well as some family favorites: *You can't control yourself around food. You'll always fail at weight loss. Sugar's a great substitute for love.* When I reflect on these messages, which I encourage you to do with your equivalent internalized negative teachings, I land on the question, *Did they bring you any joy?* The answer, not surprisingly, is a resounding No.

I hope your scripts are more benign, and that they have not hobbled you deeply or long. Either way, it's important to recognize them, so you can see when they pop up, nudge, or shove you in one direction or another. Your messaging may be very different, but it's worth taking time to think about what it is and how it's impacted you. Even once you've evaluated and accepted or rejected these scripts, you need to acknowledge how they impacted your psyche and life choices. Every time you stop singing, making art, or dancing, each time you stop trying to learn math or science, competing in a sport, applying for a prize, or even stop enjoying cookies, those voices win. There's an excellent deconstruction of this process in a book called *Art and Fear*, which looks at all the ways that we keep ourselves not merely from success but from even trying. It's worth asking that deceptively simple question, *What would you attempt if you could not fail?* Yes, asking it today, and seeing not just what you answer now, but how many other answers come knocking.

Hooray if you're ready, however overdue it may seem, to peel back the layers. If you're not, remind yourself that inside you, along with all the pieces you're afraid to look at, are big chunks of courage and resilience that you rely on without even realizing that you do so. They're so fundamental that they've steered you capably through most of life. But when you're feeling terrified or confused it's easy to forget about them.

I once worked with a counselor who used a method called Integrated Family Systems. The premise is that we're each a constellation of sub-personalities in various forms of development. Some are strong, loving, and evolved; they're the ones we'd prefer be in charge. But we've all got others, frozen in some damaged state, often from youth, though we are not immune to new hurts even as we age. In her system, your wiser-now-you talks to your younger-wounded-you and says, "Hey, listen up. It may have been so very hard then but it worked out okay. Hang in there. I promise you it gets better. Here's a hint or two and a big hug. Remember to breathe."

For this work I used the image of an old sailing vessel that showed up one day in a meditation. I was both charmed and surprised at how apt it seemed. I imagined all the miscreants, gremlins big and small, and the inner wounded ones, below deck and out of sight. I couldn't see very well into the murky dark, even using breathing techniques or tears. But I knew that the important monsters lay not in the metaphorical seas outside, but in the depths of my own psyche. I thank myself regularly for doing my deep emotional house cleaning, even when I was afraid or didn't like it, and for my counselor's warmth and skill. Having a safe place to process matters so very much. If you don't have one, keep looking.

Every piece of you that lands in the hold weighs you down and slows your progress. It takes an incredible amount of energy to keep your gremlins suppressed. Out of sight, though not out of mind. I know mine and I'd bet real money you know yours. The secrets you've covered over with good words and deeds and hope no one can remember. The pieces you buried so far below that no one can hear them scream their fear, defiance, or even vows of atonement, sincere or feigned.

What I learned from unshackling my gremlins is this: the ship of self will not keel over. Your life won't founder. Even if it heads in the wrong direction for a while, if you are sincerely committed to feeling more whole, and to saying "no more pain" to those voices, you will heal. In the interim, your loving friends, your spirit guides, and your faith and hopes for a better future will keep you from falling off the edge.

There's much more happiness to be had. Also clarity, energy, and fun. But doing this work is a necessary part of the process. It doesn't happen fast. It takes answering hard questions, time, and perhaps a trained ally. For a fabulous giant first step, begin with Brené Brown's work. She's a brilliant researcher into vulnerability who's written books and offers many online classes, podcasts, and videos. Follow her threads for many useful links and exercises, and to other excellent teachers.

No matter what, you'll have to go into the dark places. You'll have to listen for the quiet, often elusive, heartbeat of your woundings. Go visit the ones that have been hiding for decades, afraid to be seen, afraid they'll be hurt again. You have to sit with each of them and give them time to feel safe enough to talk with you. When these parts speak, you have to lean in and give them airtime, really listen, even when you'd rather flee. You have to cry with them, bear witness, and hold each of them with generosity and compassion, offering love, forgiveness, and safe harbor.

If you give these fragmented parts enough light and air, amazing things happen. You learn that everyone can be on deck and unafraid. Your gremlin selves and your holy selves. Your wise ones and your innocents. Your hopeful, trusting parts, the curious and the wary ones, and the ones that keep life orderly and safe. No one will grab the wheel and steer you towards rocks or shipwreck. Your vessel will feel lighter and livelier. It's like seeing a cloudy sky part, and the North Star appearing like a beacon. You find your way home.

Which parts of you feel fully integrated? How did you heal what used to hurt or make you afraid?

Could you speak your secrets: whatever about yourself feels immutably bad or whatever you've done that you wish you could undo?

Can you imagine a space where each got a turn to say what hurt them, what they're afraid of, or what they think you should be afraid of, other than of seeing them out in the open?

What do you imagine would happen if others could see them? What are you most afraid of?

Could you do that if I promised it really mattered?

(Are you ready for a break? Perhaps a cookie or three? You are not alone.)

SECTION 3

RISKING CHANGE

He used to say we all had a compass inside of us and what we needed to do was to find it and to follow it.
—ANN PATCHETT, STATE OF WONDER

You just can't fly when you're wearing socks, and shoes, and coats, and pants, and underwear. Everything has to go.
—PEMA CHÖDRÖN

Vocabulary Lessons

My father lived on three continents and spoke six languages. I've studied five, but English is the only one in which I can communicate nuance or depth. In college, vocabulary lessons involved a night-owl roommate who, long before her midnight snack, would pry *Russian 101* from my sleepy grasp and turn off the light. Words you learn through force-feeding rarely stick.

Some are universal, like your first "Maaaa." Two-year olds everywhere seem hardwired for "No!," whether it's in English or Urdu. And while I can't say "ice cream" in more than a few, I recognize the first-lick smile in every language. Some words are regional. I'm from Philly, so despite proper parenting epithets are intrinsic to my speech. (My favorite Philly joke: Q: How do you say the alphabet in Philly? A: Effing A, Effing B, Effing C…)

With age we learn words of connection, comfort, understanding, and caring. Also words of sorrow, judgment, guilt, and regret. Words can set memories throbbing, move us to laughter or tears, or evoke deep feelings. Words shorten the distance between people, though context matters greatly.

We've all had our heart shredded when *love* was left unspoken and *like* used instead.

I talk and write in contractions, use vernacular and slang, and lapse into cursing when I am frustrated or angry. I'm becoming shamefully lazy using emojis. But I admire the elegance of language the way I do the instructive beauty of mathematical symbols. Words can put us on our knees with simple truths and elegant pairings.

Some words become as natural as hand waving. One for me is *grok*, from *Stranger In a Strange Land*. Grok is about understanding something completely in the *I hear you, I feel you, I know into the marrow of my bones* sense. You either grok me or you don't. I love the ones I grok; I grok the ones I love.

When I share stories, the room fills with imaginary landscapes. I wave one way for a *Yes, please* outcome, while pointing off yonder can mean a very different world. We and our besties can know hard truths without words; the heart fills in what we sometimes cannot speak. Even with a Vulcan mind meld, words are only data. Feeling is what makes you grok it.

We're about to set out on a cosmic road trip. The three Hebrew words below are direct links to a special kind of knowing. Like one of Jack's magic beans they can catapult you into a different realm where you have access to much deeper knowing. Give them a quiet place and some breaths between them. Let them guide you as we shift into the transitions we have come together to face.

HAMAKOM

Hamakom is the place where time stops. Where you realize it already did and you can't remember when or how long you've felt this way. It translates to "the place." *Hamakom* is when all is still and all is well and all is right with the world. To paraphrase Walter White, you're not just in the zone, you are the zone.

For creatives, *hamakom* is when your hands can't move fast enough, and art comes in and through you. Athletes, monks, and gamblers all have their zones. It's the land of no questions or answers: pure being. In *hamakom* you don't thrash around. The world just is. You're not responsible for how things turn out or even trying to aim or shape them. You're just you at your best, in time-bending simplicity.

You can invite *hamakom* or try to conjure it. Most folks use meditation, prayer, or ritual, but no matter how you get there, in *hamakom* you're fully present. No struggle or contradiction. You have vision and a calm sense of supreme clarity. Sit with that for a moment and revel in the beautiful simplicity.

HINEINI

Hineini means "I am here." As in, "I am present and accounted for." But also, "I've fully shown up. I'm paying attention. I'm ready."

You say *hineini* when you make a big commitment. When you say yes to a new school, job, or city, let alone a wedding "I do." *Hineini* is a Bible word, used in the sacrifice of Isaac story. Moses says *hineini* at the burning bush when he agrees to free his people from slavery. *Hineini* should be the first big step on any journey. When you say *hineini*, you're not thinking about the past or future. There's no equivocation. You're fully ready and willing to say, "Yes, I'm here," and then move in whatever direction is required, even if it sounds utterly terrifying.

Where *Hamakom* is receptive, *Hineini* is active. You're a unique you, not merged with all there is. In *Star Trek, hineini* would be after beaming down and the atoms of self have re-aligned in the landing zone. *Hineini* implies complete trust and surrender to what the universe has in store for you. That's how deep *hineini* goes. It's been brewing in your soul for life-times. It's when you decide you're ready to fully show up: to change from what you've known or been into your next, presumably better, you.

Hineini is: *I am here. Amidst the chaos, mystery, and beauty of this world, I am here. I accept what is being asked of me. I am ready. I say Yes.*

Hineini is the *Yes* you are preparing to say.

KAVANAH

Kavanah means intention. It's the kind of commitment you make in the marrow of your bones. It implies an oath or vow, one that might change later after long and serious reconsideration, but not just because big or unforeseen obstacles appear on your path. It's about choosing a direction for your heart.

A *kavanah* is a serious decision made in a serious way, after lots of preparation, even if from the outside that getting ready might look like lots of pacing, hemming and hawing, and trying every other possible option first and perhaps repeatedly.

Decades ago I lived in a Los Angeles canyon. In my impa-tience to pass a tourist bus and get home, I stomped on the gas pedal so hard I popped the accelerator spring. I heard a giant roar as my car zoomed to maximum RPMs. It took all my energy to steer the narrow, winding, road, until by reflex I turned hard down my street, an even narrower path down the canyon wall. Hurtling downhill I tried every button and dial within reach ("Everything but the key...," as my kindly rescuer pointed out later). Before crashing into a fence (instead of sailing to the canyon floor), I made a deep *kavanah*: I promised to do whatever I had come into this life to do. To say *Yes, hineini* when the moment came.

When you start any big process it's wise to set a *kavanah*. A *kavanah* is more than a material goal. It implies acceptance of an unknown path and an unknown outcome. You can ask for what you want, but it may come in a form that's not as you imagined. It may require unanticipated sacrifices or extra doses of courage, or come with big unintended consequences. One does not make a *kavanah* lightly.

There are times I think that's all there is. Just completely grokking those three words. Finding the space where you can be all at once: fully present, fully committed, fully at peace. In the you-niverse I want to live in, you can have all three. It's not easy, and like other spiritual arts, requires seemingly infinite practice and patience. But at the end of the day, that's what this journey is about. It's about showing up, hearing the softest inner voice talking to the tenderest place in you, and making a commitment to change. If this book could take you anywhere, that's where I'd have it lead.

For each question below write the first seven things that you think of. No need for syntax or grammar. Just grab whatever mish-mosh comes knocking. (Three or five is fine, by the way.)

Hamakom: What's your zone? How do you get there? Do you have special practices when you are in the zone? What's different after?

Hineini: How and when do you really show up? Is it for others? For yourself?

Kavanah: What in your life do you very deeply wish to change? Are you ready to set your intention?

Extra credit: Ask to find the exquisite balance between intentionality and receptivity. Bookmark that feeling whenever it happens, because that's your new home base. Take all the time you need.

Karma Road

Most of us grew up with questing stories: rescue the maiden; slay the monster; find the grail. All allegories for a path to self-discovery that Joseph Campbell called "the hero's journey." In classical fairy tales, the journey is often a mission to solve a riddle, find a treasure, or some other grand allegory. In eastern spirituality and monastic traditions it's most like *hamakom,* a search for enlightenment or union with the divine. No matter the details, the journeyer endures challenges and tests and is transformed, to the joy and acclaim even of those who had doubted.

Many aspirants fail, even highly committed ones. In Judaism we're told of four rabbis who went to seek God. Learned men all, adept at reasoning and prayer. One goes mad; ones dies; one renounces; and only one becomes enlightened. I'd say your odds are better, as most of us are aiming for less grandiose goals. But there are so many ways to stumble or fall short of what we aspire to.

Similar imagery occurs in tarot, a prognosticating tool and the origin of modern playing cards. Instead of a hero, the protagonist is called the fool, shown as an androgynous youth dancing on a high cliff, one foot suspended over the edge, a playful pup nipping at heel. It's that acute moment before change, when it is almost inevitable, whether you choose to leap, are pushed, or just fall. The fool's card is first but is unnumbered. Your Jewish Fairy Godmother's first commandment is, *Ask for what you want.* But the hidden one is commandment zero, *Figure out what you want so you can ask for it.*

The journey of making change requires the focused commitment of the hero and the trust and innocence of the fool. Change is among the hardest things humans do, right up there with saying our final goodbyes to a loved one.

Among the reasons we're so fascinated with babies is that they hold all of life's potential, and we have not a clue what will happen to them. There's a great Chinese sci-fi novel called *The Three-Body Problem* that works its way from first alien contact to eleven-dimensional string theory. That's how open, vast, and complex life's diverse possibilities can feel. We operate in just four dimensions, and that's plenty intricate for most of us.

Our work is about paths taken and paths still ahead of you. In Helen's Cosmic Web, anywhere can lead to anywhere if you've got the right juice: a fabulous combo of desire, timing, and luck. Here's the nasty fine print: If you don't choose change, you're implicitly choosing to stay where you are, that is, stuck. There's always more to do after the biggest decision, choosing to change, but that is the necessary step. Life can shift around you, but for you to transform in a serious way, you need to choose to invite change into your life. That can feel like jumping off a cliff or like trying to fly, depending on your attitude.

Alexandra David-Néel was a Frenchwoman who traveled incognito in the closed kingdom of 1920s Tibet. She wrote many books including *The Power of Nothingness,* in which a monk goes on a quest to find the man who murdered his teacher and stole a valuable turquoise. You're with him in every possible life adventure: travels, marriages, careers, and crime solving. At the very end (spoiler alert) he wakes from his afternoon meditation. That's what the inside of your head can feel like as you imagine what your life would be if you take that first step toward change.

Think about what you most often trip over in life: Relationship? Health? Career? Addiction? Money? Is there one you'd offer up for sacrifice? Put on the altar of change and say, " @#$%&! it, let's do this! I'm ready to rewrite this story." Pick one that really matters to you and use it with the exercises in these chapters.

These issues organize how we see the world and how we operate in it. Sometimes we get stuck in how we see our stories and how we see ourselves in them. Doing that can end up creating entrenched patterns that limit the ways we interact and the possibilities we strive to manifest. Some Southwest Native American cultures have a lovely image of a maiden holding newly ripened corn and baskets of seeds—fecundity and grace with all the promise of womanhood. Imagine if you offered yourself boundless potential and a harvest of success instead of your old tropes.

It's not like archery in summer camp. You're aiming for a future you cannot see, for a you that you haven't yet become. Your transformation process will be fun some times, but a hard slog others. Change means putting one foot in front of the other even on days when you cannot bear the idea of morning. The whole point is learning to trust yourself more, because then you'll actually get somewhere new, not just talk about wanting to. One promise I can make: change will happen. You may not get fully to goal, but I believe with all my heart that you are capable of being more successful than you've been, and more easily, and becoming happier as you try.

Part of the learning is holding on less tightly to how you've always done things. Ditto for scraping back your protective layers, risking the scary places and the hard conversations you've been dodging. It may require saying *No* when you're used to saying *Yes* (or *Yes* when you're used to saying *No*), and learning delayed gratification, courage, patience, discipline, and a zillion other virtues.

This journey is not linear or predictable. It's a series of micro-moments. The decisions we make in each moment help us to raise or lower the odds of what might come next, and help determine the speed and comfort of our efforts, as well as their likelihood of success.

In my simplistic quantum theory, we're each our own micro-universe. Though we generally feel similar thrills and hurts, we're not on the same road other than the one called human. My broken heart and yours both feel sad and lousy, but we're each learning slightly different lessons, shaded by our personal history, and how we experience and roll with it. What joins us on this road is a thread of grace: that interweaving of joys and pain as we struggle and are wounded, heal and try again. We are connected by the tears and laughter we share, and the knowing we feel as we witness one another, each in our uniquely fallible way, trying to navigate the messy lessons life imposes.

We ache; we yearn; we suffer. And slowly and inexorably, we try again, praying progress will come without or please-God-at-least-with-a-little-less bruising. At our core we are creatures of hope. Hero, fool, or both at once, we search for hope and pray she returns our embrace.

This road isn't paved or straight, easy or clear. Flat stretches and occasional oases there will be, yes, but then rocky and unpredictable challenges. Sudden chasms. Scary things lurking: monsters, seducers, trickster guides, blinding storms. They can come at you fast, with only brief respites to catch your breath, let alone opportunities for any deep reflection. Unless you mean those long, dull periods. The kind where nothing at all seems to change, until you realize that you must, or you'll keep walking in circles.

This journey requires stripping down to the essentials. Not all at once, and not necessarily through punishment or abnegation. But saying *Yes* to this road means asking hard questions, and pushing hard for answers. On the good days you'll feel the wind at your back. Hard ones may require all the grit of childbirth. Self-knowing is hard, whether it's a meditation retreat or climbing a tall mountain. Before, we may be afraid or unsure. After, there's a sense of purification, victory over something that felt difficult or dark and that kept us feeling less than who we really are.

The hero's journey requires tending your soul with the same attention you'd give a summer garden: preparation, weeding, and waiting, with almost certainly some loss before the harvest. It helps not to be in a rush, and to savor anticipation like a special new treat. It's a tough road. But it's worth it.

What if you felt your life was a sweet and nourishing journey?

What gives you that kind of hope? Can you recall those moments?

What's your default attitude about change? What if you were optimistic and trusting, instead of pessimistic or annoyed?

What if life was a series of joys and surprises? What if that's the journey we're on, instead of how it feels on cold or crappy days? What if that's the road inviting you? Would you take the next step?

Mapmaking

We live in a world of intention, whether we're conscious of it or not. I'd mangle any theory of physics I'd try to explain, but the idea of a multi-verse—different simultaneous configurations of what folks in each think of as reality—is pretty close to how I see the world. I'm glad there's more science and story about this in our time: wonderful new theories that the universe itself is conscious; that we're each small, breathing parts of it; and that there are alternative parallel universes, with variations on us in each of them. Science catching up to spirituality and metaphysics, hooray.

Would that I could see that cosmos unfolded the way I could my father's map on a family road trip: the red lines and the blue ones, all pointed to a clear goal (and as far as I can tell, more reliable than GPS). I'm like everyone else, stumbling around in the dark, trying to find the right path, or at least a little more light. For a good, fun read on this, grab Blake Crouch's physics thriller *Dark Matter*. It points towards home with a vivid combo of heart and head, and makes clear that mapping a path to your preferred you-niverse isn't like ordering off the "create your best world now" menu.

Yes, you're a co-creator of how your lessons get taught. But no, not every piece of crap that comes at you is because you somehow wished it, consciously or not. Yes, karma spins the wheels, but it's not as clear as in a movie-of-the-week story. Karma is a bigger picture than most of us can glimpse, let alone understand. We're here in our be-here-now reality, more than enough for most of us, getting through today, tomorrow, and next week.

Our lives are so very much in motion. Daily lives are busy. If you up the ante to tornado, tsunami, or flood, normal life is upended. In a war or crisis, when not all are alive, we become a world of emigrants and immigrants. When it's *What do I take with me?* the stakes go way up. And to whom goes the luck and burden of surviving a catastrophe?

I heard a great story about teaching people what refugees face. The instructor laid a couple dozen printed cards on a table and said to the participants: "Soon a bell will ring. You will have thirty seconds to decide which five cards to take with you. And then we leave this room." The cards included: Passport and identity papers. Medicine. Money. Food. Blanket. Water. A cooking pot. Prosthetics. Your child's favorite toy. Your pet.

As we proceed along our journeys, metaphorical and real, we lose even each of these, one by one or faster. To bandits or bribery, trickery or thievery. At the end of the road there's just you, and if you're lucky those you love have made it too. No matter how good our maps or how clear our intentions, no matter how well we think we've planned our journey, there will always be surprises. Difficulties we couldn't anticipate, things that will delay, threaten, or harm us, and almost certainly change us.

There will be times you simply want to turn around. Just want to say "uncle," give up and go home, to be where it's warm, safe, and known, and you feel enfolded like snuggling into fleece on a chilly afternoon. But like the proverbial trail of breadcrumbs eaten by hungry birds, there is no road back. You're on the path and have already begun to morph—so has the road. The journey has chosen you. The only way out is forward and through.

It's best to stay alert, attentive, and aware. Pay close attention to your inner voice as well as the outer context. Being even a little prescient is a wonderful boon. I think doing the prompts and processes I'm suggesting enhances intuition, but perhaps that's congenital optimism. Think about the big picture and what's around the next bend. Stay flexible enough to respond quickly and don't be afraid to choose what you do not know. Keep your intuition channel wide open and practice listening to what it's telling you. Rely on your growing ability to make better decisions.

If something glimmers, move toward it but not in a rash or foolhardy way. As folks are told at Country Fair, an annual Oregon craft, music, and aging-hippie fest: "Don't take food from strangers." That's a metaphor for choosing your own path and not going on someone else's trip by accident, codependence, coercion, laziness, or simply staying stuck.

If we're good and lucky we may meet allies, although we may not immediately recognize them. They can come in many forms. Stretching to know, learn, and trust them is part of the journey's teaching. You'll need discernment too, to know which ones to welcome, and which might be a trickster who'll distract you or a nemesis carrying some long-forgotten piece of karma. You'll need to trust your gut, your heart, and your head, and hope like hell they line up singing the same tune, because it's rarely pretty when they don't. You know how you shout at the screen, "No, you fool! Don't go into that dark forest!" Sigh. Would that real-life dangers were so easy to discern.

With luck and experience, you'll learn to tell a helper from a menace, though that knowing may come hard-won. What seems bright and alluring may hold harsh, even dangerous, energy. You may not realize you've blown it until you feel yourself sagging, weaker, and drained, or until a piece of you feels damaged or lost. Those nasty places require and also teach resilience. They're best appreciated by most folks, including me, in retrospect. Staying in a bad situation, be it domestic or professional, can cost you years, self-esteem, happiness, and more. But some wrong choices can cost you broken body parts, your sanity, or even your life.

Tough times are implacable but valuable teachers. I hope yours are no worse than you feel ready for. From experience I can tell you that it is possible to recover from almost every bad decision, even if it takes time, energy, and emotional resilience you didn't know you had. Sometimes we need the lesson, and all the tough stuff it brings along with it, to finally put a stubborn problem to rest. Rarely our first choice, but perhaps the last time we enact that particular wrong scenario, because sometimes the hardest taught teachings actually stick best. And as a bonus, you'll have more confidence the next time things don't go according to plan, which can feel like most of the time in some phases of our lives. When life feels like you're tumbling down Niagara Falls in a wooden barrel, remind yourself that there is a landing zone, even if it's a rough ride until you get there.

For most of us, this isn't a vacation incarnation (except perhaps for our pets). What can feel like a lot of real time for us is but a blip in the cosmosphere. Scientists tell us the universe is about five billion years old, a big number that's hard to grasp with mere mortal minds and measures. And one that should make the weekly crises that we stress over assume a different level of importance. But it doesn't seem to. They're our messes, and it matters very much to us how they resolve. But in this and every other parallel now, your soul is doing its work, learning what you're here to learn. You may get it more right or screw up more horribly in one universe or another. But these are all what Dara Horn so lovingly calls "versions" in *Eternal Life*, or "melodic variations on a theme." Good news or bad, you and all those versions of you are probably wrestling with pretty much the same issues, even if the packaging, props, and timing are different in their parallel worlds.

We're all on a journey we don't fully understand, even those who ask about it often. A learning that—unless we're facing imminent danger—emerges in fits and starts. Lucky us's get to take a bite, work on things for a while, and come back for our next chunk of teaching. The less lucky of us get tested longer and harder with little respite, few rewards, and harder chores and dangers.

That's one reason why regular rituals and practices are good: they reinforce our hard-won lessons, and remind us often of what we worked so hard to grok. Whether you call your practice meditation, journaling, working with a counselor, or regularly meeting a group of like-minded people to talk over issues or study together, having a regular form and/or forum that reinforces your goals can help you reach them. But keep in mind that rituals can sometimes become rote: they're better habits to be sure, but not a substitute for continuing to do your deep soul work, asking the tough questions and probing even deeper for the answers. Without continued vigilance about making progress we can fall into patterns, albeit newer and incrementally better ones, but still not where we truly want to land. We risk getting stuck again, and not realizing it's time to expand our repertoire of tricks and tools.

I sometimes think of life like a complex video game. There are traps and obstacles, both seen and surprising, to surmount before we reach the goals. When we solve one challenge, new sets of possibilities emerge to confront and teach us. Each of us is like Player One in our unique version of the game. We stumble, fail, and start over again (even if it takes a while to recover before we do). Even if it sometimes seems like one step forward and then two back, we learn with each try, until death do us part from this particular version of us.

This whole purpose of this process we're doing together is for you to realize your answer to the *What do you really want?* question. Always remember the map that you are making is for a life that will give you that, whatever your particular answer to the question might be. I describe the path towards greater self-knowing, authenticity, and happiness, and I am trusting you will translate those into practical manifestations for your own life. But no matter the nouns and the verbs we each choose, getting there means getting unstuck, confronting and unpacking the old stories, and becoming brave enough to risk what making the newer ones will require.

Your next steps may not necessarily be obvious from where you are today. But they're on tap, waiting for you to invite them. It helps to make that a conscious invitation. To say, *Here's the next piece of big work I am ready to tackle.* You might frame it as find a partner, lose a size, save for a house, or strengthen my faith. It can be in any dimension from material to spiritual, anywhere along the continuum you feel ready for. Failing to consciously engage with your karmic homework allows capricious fates to write the script. They might just be mischievous, but they might play with malevolence, and it's hard to tell up front what anyone else's agenda might be.

Tapping into those other you-niverses can prevent you from falling into a painful abyss. Remember that everything we're doing here can pull juice from all those parallel soul parts, each of them thrashing and struggling, too, and fueled by the same desire for light and clarity, and by *Get this done dammit this time, because there's so much more I want to do than wrestle any more with this*!

Of course we want to be the mapmaker, to draw the path and know how to get where we think we're headed, preferably without a crisis, or at worst one we can resolve. Rabbi Lawrence Kushner tells a great story about a vacation he and his wife took in a national wilderness park. As they set off for a day hike, they ask the ranger, "Are there bears there?" I imagine a laconic pause before he responds, "If I could tell you for sure there wouldn't be any bears, it wouldn't be a wilderness now would it?"

Good news for us: When you go past your safety zones you almost always learn that the Monsters Live Here sides of the map are only the edges of your consciousness. Ask anyone who's ever stopped hiding some big secret about themselves, be it sexual orientation or childhood abuse. The energy surge is potent. More importantly, your willingness to be your authentic self in the world can align you with your higher self and true purpose.

You can't prepare for every contingency. Trying to do that will keep you immobilized, like the warning, "The man who tries to write the perfect will dies without one." When I try to be ready for anything and everything, the path usually takes longer and is more complicated than when I follow my gut instincts. But I've certainly dropped into many a metaphorical ravine watching the sky instead of the path. There's a precious and sometimes precarious balance between caution and wisdom on the one hand, and courage and willingness to risk on the other.

Practice imagining a fabulous new you-niverse and moving towards it. Choose that new you-niverse with every fiber of your being, from the best and most fabulous you that you've ever felt like. And I'm serious when I say practice. I mean sit down regularly and imagine it; dress up like it and prance in front of the mirror; try out your new name, new look, new way of feeling whenever you can. Because he was convinced no one ever reads the signature on a credit card receipt, a friend tried out possible pseudonyms for his next life phase. Say hi for me if you ever encounter Eduardo Pantalones Loco; he's a fabulously happy bartender, formerly a stressed-out economist.

I don't care if you use wine or incense or tea. But I do care that you create space in your life for imagining the possibilities you want to make real. The time you spend imagining and embracing that future is reshaping the possibilities as well as preparing you. It creates a *kavanah* (a deep intention), gives you courage, and clears the path.

There are no ruby-red slippers to transport you instantly. Like the November 2016 picture of the old woman holding a sign that said, "I can't believe I still have to fight this @#$%&!," you'll need to trudge through the rain to rallies and sign endless petitions for what matters to you, and put in weeks, years, and maybe longer before you feel like you're making any progress. In personal terms that may mean pushing yourself onto the treadmill or out the door. It means saying, "No, no, no" as you drive past the bakery, and learning to enjoy what you already own instead of shopping. It means quiet evenings with your journal, writing what you feel and letting yourself cry.

If you show up and do this work day after day, making time to visualize yourself happier, you will create a map for your journey that's full of honesty and truth. You'll find both authenticity of heart and tenacity of purpose. It'll be worth it later, and maybe even sooner.

Being short, I take exceptional delight watching a small player succeed in sports. Someone who's decided that height is only a genetic artifact, and that oomph and grit can overcome what nature has seemed to limit. We can't design or predict our futures with any certitude or control. We certainly can't get all the details right. But we can go strong for tone and style, double down on attitude, heart, openness of thinking, and willingness to show up. Those are cards worth packing, and they'll serve you well in good times and in bad.

Your values will become your most reliable tools on the road to what you really want. No one can steal them, though some folks you meet may try to shift them towards their own. Take note if that happens, and question what their reasons might be. Self-knowing is the best map and the ultimate survival tool.

What should your mapmaking feel like? Flowing, rich, round, and full. Pregnant with possibility. If all you draw is a line, you'll fall off the trail pretty quickly. Think what outcomes would make you happy, regardless of specifics. Consider what warms your inside and nurtures your outside. Think texture and tone more than details. Imagine whole regions of your future where anywhere might become home. An important caveat: Don't set upper limits on what you ask for. Leave room in your goals for the universe to surprise you with bounty. At a time of great happiness, I remember thinking, *I wouldn't have had the sense to ask for this much joy.*

Make a map that feels good in every direction, one that feels like how you feel when you feel your best. Imagine not a pinprick of a world but a starburst of them. A multi-verse where you'd be happy anywhere. A place where your lessons come bite-sized and beautifully prepared. Great seasoning and flavor. Just enough adventure to be savory and none of those gnarly bits. Sure, there will be hidden roots to trip you, fields of wreckage and debris to pass through, and challenges to confront. But if you know your innards, and if you like and trust yourself, your chances of making it to goal and being happy go way up, the specifics of your day or landing zone notwithstanding.

What's most important? Knowing who you are. Knowing what matters to you. Knowing your friends and teachers, guides and allies, your communities of affiliation, of comfort, of shared visioning. Hold them close and love them. Know how to find them in the dark. Make sure they can find you. Feel safe and trust that. Wrap everything else in that and keep it with you on your path.

Keep remembering that feeling even when all the cards are gone, when bandits or storms, a bad job or a bitter relationship seems to have hijacked your journey. It's only a blink of the multi-verse away from turning around. That knowing will light your way, and help guide you to an even better world you will help to create.

This process will change you, no matter when you say yes or what you do right afterwards, as long as you continue to do the work.

When you set out to make changes, whether they're voluntary or feel imposed by circumstance, do you set an intention?

Do you make a plan before you begin, or assume you'll wing it as you go?

Do you think about what could go wrong? How do you respond when things go haywire?

How do you cope with fears of the unknown?

Find a quiet place. Think about the pattern you most want to change. Take three breath cycles and ask those questions again. Grab words, images, sensations, whatever shows up, with the usual caveat that it may not make sense to anyone except you. Park that feeling in the marrow of you. Return often to visit and affirm your intention to create the life you want to live.

Run with Me

We're complicated critters, both in our heads and in our hearts. Some days things seem sharp and clear: whom we love, and whom we'd pay never to see or hear about again; what to do, when and how. All the tools are at hand and we are ready. Other times everything seems to happen in slow motion; we go through our routines in a mild, dull haze. It's not that we're miserable, but we feel weighted in place and big decisions seem harder to make. And then there are those moments when life suddenly speeds up, when our world moves to a tipping point. Instead of leisurely contemplating our choices, we have to make decisions faster, or confront issues that we hadn't even thought about facing. This can happen when someone imposes a change on you (like a conversation that starts with "We need to talk.....") or when you're eyeball-to-eyeball with a core issue you thought was parked safely in your distant future.

A few years ago an old injury finally did its worst: I was on a Sunday walk when my knee locked up completely. I was tethered to a park bench, hobbled and humbled, unready for aging. The message was clear: All my avoidance, cleverness, glib talk, and well-used, I'll-start-my-diet-next-Monday tactics were worthless. It's like the Nature Bats Last bumper sticker, but instead it said, Sorry, Honey, Your Body Bill's Come Due. In the big picture, knees are pretty easy, but they're connected at the hip to diet and exercise.

One more chance please, I promise I'll be good! I pleaded. I suspect you know this dance.

In the moments you're about to repeat some bad choice (say another piece of cheesecake, drinking and driving, or hooking up with your ex), you tune out everyone who's screaming, *No, no, no! I don't want to clean up after that!* They're trying to knock sense into you, praying you don't blow it, again. As if you could hear them. We've all starred in that movie. AA and other addiction programs have a structure of meetings and sponsors to help folks past those moments and to pick them up when they fail. The rest of us rely on the patience and love of our friends, and the universe's inevitable, and often less charming, ways of teaching us.

Finally, in some elusive moment, by a miracle of grace, we realize that if we don't change our life right now, with this very choice, not much else will matter. We'll die pretty much how we are: older (or not), richer or poorer, good times and bad, in sickness and less health, till death do us part from this particular manifestation of us.

If reincarnation happens, we may get to come back. But that new version of us will have to start at go just to get back to the same decision. Because, until we get our karmic homework right, or at least a whole lot better, we're going to face our issues over and over and over. Yours may be whom you choose to love, what you eat, or what you do with money. The variations are infinite, but for each of us they loom large and often on our path. Let's call them your "It." Until we're willing to say and do something differently with our menu of Its, we all end up hobbled and humbled and spinning on the karmic wheel. We stay in what Judaism calls *mitzrayim,* "the narrow place," which is how Jews refer to the time of slavery in Egypt: the place of constriction, of staying stuck.

One day, like the woman who got enlightened with the splash of dough in hot oil, we're facing the choices that will get us unstuck. It's a flash of acute grace, a thunk of the highest degree. It's the proverbial come-to-Jesus moment when we're ready to hear it. In Jewish metaphor, it's standing at the shore of the Red Sea, fleeing Egypt, as we tell the tale each year, with angry chariots bearing down and roiling water straight ahead. It's walk-in-deeper-than-your-nostrils time, right now, praying hard for a miracle. Deciding to change is no Sunday stroll.

Someday I hope, whatever your It is, you'll decide to shift your patterns. That you'll take your boat of self beyond the sight of land, with all the risk and danger that implies. Towards where the map warns of monsters. To the unknown edge and past it.

Tibetan Buddhists prepare for dying. Specifically for the moment of death, that brief transition between when your soul leaves this body and you go to wherever you go. When the you that you have been isn't here anymore, but when your soul has choices that are accessible only in that narrow window between being human and whatever follows. In that instant you have access to so much more wisdom, strength, clarity, and knowing than on any given day. The guidance all says to *Go towards the light,* so I'm trusting that's right.

When I talk about deciding to change, I'm talking about an incarnated moment that seems equally and vividly clear. The time in this lifetime when you realize you are indeed ready to do what you've been wrestling with for a very long time. That you're ready to tackle what you've hoped and longed to do all the time you've been cautious, hesitant, or tried half-heartedly and gave up.

When that moment comes, try to breathe a little deeper, take in a little more oxygen, and fix a talisman in your heart for how you feel. Do whatever it takes to know your way back to there. Because even though that moment may feel like the biggest change you could possibly make, on the other side of that decision there will be more tests of your resolve. Knowing your way back to the core of your intention will give you the extra oomph and courage you'll need. You'll thank the you that launched you, the way your morning girl thanks the one who prepped coffee and lunch fixings the evening before. It's not quite like getting a superpower in a Marvel movie but that seed is there. You're evolving into a different and better you. You believe more in yourself so you're more ready for risk.

There's a great TV series called *Underground* about a group of slaves who flee a Georgia plantation, circa 1850. At the end of episode two, the smart and ready protagonist says urgently to his newfound love, "Run with me!" And then the screen goes dark. The implications are huge. He's going for it all, doesn't want to choose between freedom and love. But we hadn't seen her preparing, and suddenly her whole future rides urgently on a *Yes* or *No*.

Run with me. Run with me. Run with me. It's an eyeball-to-eyeball moment.

Colson Whitehead's *Underground Railroad* offers a painful, raw, and telling description of how difficult the road to freedom can be. He's talking specifically about slavery and racism. We're talking more metaphorically about change. But when you're feeling stuck, life can feel as if you're caged and the key is nowhere in sight. It's hiding inside you, as is most of the courage and grit you will need to get to goal.

You've lived your life pretty much as you know it. You've imagined what change might be like, perhaps even imagined how it will feel on the other side. But to actually endure the hardships of transition, to risk suffering and loss, seriously ups the ante. It deters many of us for long stretches of time. Don't beat on yourself if you feel resistance or that everyone else is moving forward and you are stuck. Everyone's process is different. But I promise you from the depth of my knowing that when you are ready to say Yes to the run-with-me question, you will have such a surge of energy and optimism that it will carry you much farther than you ever dreamed possible.

I'm always fascinated by what it takes to reach the tipping point. To say "Yes, I will run," where your "run" might be leaving a job or partner, giving up drugs or alcohol, or being brave in a way that only you understand when you talk to yourself in your most honest inner conversations. Your thinking powers, even coupled with intense desire, will not suffice. If they were enough, we'd already be enlightened and happier, perhaps generous philanthropists and wise peacemakers. Change requires will, fueled by heart and gut, plus the powerful knowing that only you can start the process. But what makes all that come together is hard to predict.

Most of us, and all we know, have light-years more freedom than a slave, a refugee, or a person who's homeless or lives with food insecurity, to name but a few. But even in our least comfortable days, we're victims of giving ourselves permission to stay as we are. Victims of the easy familiarity of defaulting to our known—by custom, addiction, or fear of change, even if that known is very bad for us. Things that do us harm and keep us stuck often give swift and delicious satisfaction. Think sugar or cocaine for a range of quick highs, each with its own damaging consequences. Doing things differently rarely feels good very quickly, and not reliably for what can seem like eons. The first step towards freedom often tastes like harsh medicine. Until it doesn't.

The only thing I know for sure is this: there's no hiding. If you don't face your issues this round, you'll inevitably face them again. And again. Sooner or later, probably often, likely with more and more hassle every cycle. It happens in this lifetime on a regular basis. It may happen whatever way souls work through their karma. I'm okay not knowing the mechanics, though I'll always choose the hope of atonement, redemption, and another chance to get it right.

As much as we loathe our bondage, we often struggle long and hard before we free ourselves: lots of twisting and turning, two steps forward and one step back, many times and again, before that ultimate decision. Before saying *Yes, I'll run,* not knowing what will come, but recognizing that nothing after will be the same.

We get chances to make things different. But to take them we have to be willing to release old crap, not look back to see if it still needs us or to admit we still need it. Like Lot's wife, we must at all costs avoid turning around. We need to be ready, committed, and sure-footed on our new path, and not carry guilt over the past with us on our journey.

Change happens in chunks as life unfolds. When folks graduate, change cities, start new jobs, have a child. Marriage too, though love's optimism can act like high tide. Those commitments and adventures keep us busy, productive, useful, loving, and loved. We have family, friends, teams, parties, and all the frills that make it easy to stay where we are, comfortable in the familiar. They make it easier to avoid the tough stuff locked away in those littlest dolls, the stuff that keeps knocking at the edges of your psyche, asking for attention.

Change means saying *Yes* to something you don't know how to do, that you're afraid you might fail at, and would prefer not hurt. You need to risk every possible form failure can take. Your imagination will supply lots of scary scenarios, because even if your body feels like a prisoner, your mind is not. Every chance you give it, your mind will try to distract, delay, and deter you by spinning difficult and lurid scenarios. They'll only frighten and distract you. Transcending them is a necessary part of the process. It won't last forever, unless you become too afraid, which is implicitly choosing *No, I'll stay stuck.*

Your time to choose is coming. Never forget, whatever we imagine gets an extra oomph of probability. Like batters with balls hurled towards them at ninety-five mph, you may have to decide quickly what to do next. Whether on a hunch or just out of desperation, when a good chance comes, swing strong and sure, with a beautiful arc of intention. Be ready to run. It's clear in baseball, but less so in life, where the 24/7 lassitude of days lulls us into opaque and dutiful submission.

The biggest question of this book is how you'll answer your unique version of *Run with me…*

I'm asking you to go deeper than the current form of your life. I'm asking you about a soul commitment, a *hineini* of fully showing up for a new life. I'm asking you to choose change even when you fear you have no idea what you're doing or what will happen on the other side.

Even after your first *Yes*, life will send you many more chances to choose. I hope they will be easier, but there's no guarantee. You'll find strength you never knew you had, and allies you might never have envisioned, in strangers and friends alike. Your guides will watch over you and lend a hand. Remember to ask for help whenever you're unsure or afraid. No one powers through life's toughest transitions on their own. Asking for help is a sign of commitment, not of weakness.

This process will change you, no matter when you say Yes, or what you do immediately after saying it, as long as you continue to take actions and move in the direction of your Yes.

You will emerge leaner, dirty, and perhaps scarred, but with new light, fierceness, freedom, and a surprisingly silly smile. Plus a sense of who you are that you cannot see from here. You'll like her and be proud, even if that's hard to believe from the before side of Yes.

Alexandra David-Néel told of an initiation she witnessed in her travels with Tibetan lamas. The old lama escorts the acolyte across the high plains by moonlight. His instructions are clear: "I'm going to whack you on the head, cut you into pieces, and throw them into that fire. Please reassemble yourself before I return at dawn." For years I took it literally. But even as metaphor it is potent and vivid.

What could be harder than what that acolyte faced? What keeps you from saying Yes and meaning it?

Leap of Faith

There will come a moment, or if you are lucky perhaps a stream of moments, when you are suffused with all the joy, pride, and intention that you have glimpsed and felt before. You will have a solid sense of trust in yourself and your decision-making. You will feel your Yes in every part of you: body, mind and soul.

Those moments are like a magical passage to another universe where whatever's left to be healed improves almost without effort. When you come back to the who and now, or perhaps a click or two of the cosmos further on, you stand a little taller, and are more trusting in your gut that things are going to be okay, certainly better, and maybe even good.

When that happens, keep it close to your heart. A leap of faith may not fill you with certainty, because those magic moments vanish and our very messy human qualities of doubt and second-guessing rush in to fill the void. In those times we can make foolish, even rashly foolish, decisions just to quell the competing voices in our heads. If you've done your homework, you'll see what's happening and recover much more quickly than when you were less aware. Like an Olympian at the starting gate, you have prepared yourself. You may not win the race, but you'll know you deserve to be in it.

I've always been a journaler. All the things I tell myself a zillion times, that my friends and guides are hoarse from shouting, get captured in illegible scribbles and forgotten abbreviations. The writing of it matters more than the recollecting. My favorite style of journals have inspirational quotes from folks like Rilke, Lao-Tzu, and Thich Nhat Hanh. Every so often the one I pull from my stash has a quote often attributed to Anaïs Nin: "The day came when the risk to remain tight in a bud was more painful than the risk it took to blossom." It's like the universe has fired a shot over my bow and given me fair warning: *Time to jump,* the way urgent life-saving warnings like *RUN! Run NOW!* are given in Netflix's *Stranger Things,* appearing on a wall-sized Ouija board created for messages from The Upside Down.

Recess is over. The time for procrastination is past. As the old saying goes, it's time to poop or get off the pot. If you're serious about saying *Yes,* apply the Nike maxim: Just Do It. If you're not, ask yourself what's nailed your feet to the floor. Consider going back to the exercises you skipped and doing them, or call your best friend for a walk and a talk. The inner work matters, and so do your actions. One without the other shortchanges your chances for success.

It's rare for any of us to start making these big changes without some deep motivation. We usually change from a push or a pull. Some are vivid and immediate. On Nov 9, 1939 in Germany, on a night now called *Kristallnacht*, thousands of Jewish shop windows were broken: clouds of shards that presaged clouds of ash. Violence and abuse, angry mobs yelling "Get out!," and a frightened nation watching mute and afraid. That's what November 2016 felt like in the United States, at least for liberals, with all our fears of what worse would follow. The work of generations swept away in a neo-con putsch, festooned with blooms of swastikas. I thought about moving to Canada, following my immigrant lineage to a new land. Getting that far, even if just in thought, was like lifting one foot over the edge.

That's the leap of faith part. Being willing to go, to say *Yes*, even when you haven't the faintest idea of what will follow. You can plan, you can hope, and you can pray. But all your organizing and hoping gets tossed into life's fragile mix of fate and free will, dumb luck or bad luck, and being in the right or wrong place at the right or wrong time. None of us knows what the future holds, even if we wish very, very hard that we could or have the hubris to think we do.

What followed for me was letting go of stuff. Not in any nuanced way, touching everything only once. More of a cu-rated divesting, closet by drawer. Clothes and shoes to the women's shelter, a family of refugees, and the homeless. A recycling bin of paper. The rest to thrift shops, art schools, and friends. I heard an echo of the death camps: *To the left, death. To the right, life.* I felt lighter and leaner after. Readier, but still planted.

The *Run with me* question was still there, letting me play my games while I stalled for time. Dispassionately distant some of the time, looming and challenging others. *Yes* or *No*, not in each discarded item, but in the process. It hung with me like a penitent seeking sanctuary, until I welcomed it in, to sit with the question instead of running from it. To give it true honor and weight, even if I wasn't ready to answer. Even that wasn't easy. The idea of leaving my heart folk, a town I could navigate in the dark, and a home that had cocooned my evolution and growth made the answer easy: *Bolt the door and leave me alone!* That's a solid *NO!* The other answer: *Yes, I'm ready.* But I wasn't.

Remember the fool with one foot dangling in the nanosecond of suspension, the moment before decision. That's a great time to find your inner sense of balance. Perhaps practice your yoga tree pose. Learn how to be so solid, so still, and so willing to be present that nothing can knock you off center. That consciousness will help you greet your next phase of evolution with anticipation and excitement.

When a "volunteer" plant appears in our garden, the gift of a bird or squirrel, for a while we don't know what it is. Early on it's hard to distinguish between weed and flower. We have to let it tell us on its own schedule. You can ask a friend if she knows or watch with bemused curiosity until you do. Creeping vetch or another intruder, it's an easy good-bye. If it's a flower, you help it along. In the world of souls, such a seed might become anything. An astronaut or doctor, teacher or musician. A person of achievement, creativity, and impact, or a loving friend or neighbor. Or, sadly, a refugee on the run. Best to embrace each, hoping its bloom will help rebuild what has been shattered in every holocaust and genocide. Best to nurture all the lives and their potential for kindness and peace.

Every time you get a gift from the universe, whether it's watching your child's dance recital or the scent of a blooming rose, remember to say "Thank you." Because in that moment of stillness, you will hear the answer you may have been reluctant to give, the *Yes* that is ready to be heard. In the amazing calculus of the soul something has shifted. You're outside the tumult of thinking, can feel the simple grace that is calling you, and inviting you to move towards it.

Every nanosecond's a little different than the last or next. Even if human sense organs can't tell, below the drumbeat of our heart, on some cellular level, just asking the *Run with me* question plants a seed that grows in you. Whether you nurture it with vision or drown it in fear, it's going to keep touching the edges of your consciousness. Cell by cell, moment by moment, it will change you. But until you have readiness in the marrow of you, in that magic moment of now, you won't choose *Yes*.

Choosing *Yes* or *No* is the crossroads.

In very early thirteenth century southern France there was a sect of Christians named the Cathars. They believed in direct communication with the divine (as in who needs a Pope or Church). Sophy Burnham's *The Treasure of Montsegur* is a great novel about this period. The Cathars lived simply; spiritually they had much in common with their Kabbalastic neighbors. Both were targets of the Inquisition. Instead of being burned at the stake, hundreds of Cathars held hands and leapt off cliffs, still to die, but with choice and intention.

I hope you have no such force compelling you, and that you get to decide when your change is ripe. Don't let whatever's behind you spook you into falling. Take as long as you need. Start small: each time you notice a shift, notice that you noticed, that your inner voice spoke, even if it was a whisper. Those whispers will get louder and more compelling. Really feel this, so when you say *Yes*, you say it in thirty-six point type. Make your commitment so complete there's no going back. Just forward to places unknown, sure-footed and strong, even though you don't yet know what comes next. There will come that moment.

If you are unsure, or encounter early difficulties, don't be shy about asking for help. Early in my spiritual journey, I learned acupressure. One day, while giving a session, I heard myself spontaneously praying. Instead of fretting if I had the acu-points exactly right, I'd been asking the unseen for healing, trusting my hands to do their work while I opened energy channels through me and my client. To whom or what was I praying?

My spiritual dynamics are a mix of mysticism and humanism, plus stubborn trust in the evolving goodness of the human heart. Even at the peak of my return to Judaism, I cared about Torah mostly as a metaphor for personal development. Before, during, and after, I have unequivocally believed in connecting with energies beyond human sense perceptions, and in the benefit of regularly making time to access them. Most folks call that prayer.

Prayer is a place to give gratitude and to be humbler. We pray because we recognize that the cosmos is a big place, and our desires probably aren't the epicenter. I certainly hope they're not. I regularly ask for guidance, and try to remember to say thanks when I feel guided, unless I've just stubbed my toe, when I'm as profane as any drunken sailor. Prayers are what matter after you strip away all the extras. It's what Anne Lamott discusses so beautifully in *Help, Thanks, Wow: Three Essential Prayers*. Certainly that's when most folks pray, no matter what words they use or what direction they aim.

Almost everyone has a way of connecting with something greater than themselves, whether it's walking in nature or singing in a choir. It's important to commune regularly with whatever you honor as divine, timeless, and more knowing, using whatever rituals feel most right to you. Whatever gives you a sense of trust in the universe is important to honor. It is not a substitute for self-knowing, for right living, or simple compassion and kindness. And your prayers have no greater moral authority than do anyone else's. Many religions, regardless of their views on divinity, teach the same simple truth: treat others as you wish to be treated. The problem is where the lines are drawn around who is other. Imagine human history without one religion oppressing others to convince them whose god is better or stronger. What might we now be as a planet?

I believe in prayer as active practice. Not so much in the "gimme" sense of kids wishing for holiday gifts, but rather inviting outcomes for everyone's best and highest good. For example, when the house next door was for sale, I prayed for quiet, gentle neighbors. For my struggles with sugar, that I remember the pause button. For this book, that it be clear and true. And for my aging cat, a life of heath and safety, and that she pass easily. I'd wish that last for us all.

Think about the changes you truly want to make in your life. Invite prayers without worrying about a specific form. Try this even if you are a professed atheist, because prayer isn't about a deity. It is about framing your intention for what sector of the universe you want to find yourself travelling in.

Prayers will come to you unbidden after you open that door. When they do, write them in the simplest way you can: a few clear images and hopes for every part of your life.

They will form an intention that prepares your path. They will clarify your inner world and help shape the map that guides you. Pay close attention to what rings most true, even if it sometimes surprises you. All of this is part of your Yes.

Crossing the Bridge

I want to clearly disavow the No Pain No Gain school of progress. Life shouldn't hurt any more than it does on any given
day. Too often we associate change with pain. We prefer to
burrow in, wanting our lives to feel like a snow day: comfy
and warm, snuggled with a good book and a cup of cocoa. It's
natural to drift. Mostly we're content to let evolution happen
slowly. Not rocking the boat is a lesson we learn young. We
prefer going with the flow to challenging or disrupting it. That
theory works until your stasis stops being comfortable or safe.

When we're motivating ourselves, or seriously pressed,
we see glimmers of something different on the far horizon.
Newer, brighter, cleaner, maybe with that new-car smell.
But it's more than just sensory bait. Something inside you
has declared herself ready. It might start out as a small voice,
easy to miss in the clank and clutter of the day. Or it might
sometimes say *Hello!* so loudly and quickly that you want to
slam the door. Either way, you'll say *Hello* back when you're
ready, and probably not a moment before.

In Jewish mysticism there's a rabbi of legend, Nachman of
Breslov, a travelling story and parable teller. He's a Zen koan

kind of teacher, who instructs by making you scratch your head and take a deeper look at yourself and the world around you. Among his most famous teachings: "Life is but a narrow bridge. What is important is not to be afraid." Hopefully, you're already looking deeper, scratching your psyche more, plus doing more of what you need to, with less fretting and more focusing. Maybe you're even starting to enjoy the idea that you're readier for change. You'll still need confidence, caution, and respect for what you're attempting. I'll always pick a short drop over a scary one if given half a choice. But life doesn't always let us choose. Change can require a level of courage and commitment that may take a while to muster, but it can also be thrust upon us in ways and at times that leave us no choice.

It's worth making time for a life inventory, asking which parts of your life you want to keep until you die, which you wish would change, and which you're afraid you're stuck with. Invite the more evolved and supportive parts of you to come help. You might be surprised at how many parts you genuinely like, even if you feel disappointed about the ones you feel stuck with. The parts you like, appreciate, even rely on, are on tap whenever you need them, though too often when we're wriggling like a fish on a line we forget about them. These strengths will come in handy when the bridge gets narrow or you are confronted with unexpected challenges. Also, never forget change is hard work. It's fine to promise yourself a reward for doing what you're doing. Happiness promotes more happiness, and change doesn't have to feel bad or hurt, despite our fears. Sometimes it's even fun, though that idea is hard to believe on the getting ready side. In fact, you'll know you're really crossing the bridge when being bold starts to feel more exciting.

Even if your "doing" has only been reading the questions in this book and cruising on by, thinking you'll do the meditating and journaling later, the biggest part of true doing is letting the questions in. Each time you do, some small door opens inside you. It's like taking a handi-wipe to your *klipot*, the layers that cover your inner light, that divine spark in you. It may seem like it's only a knock on spirit's door saying, "Hey, you got a sec?" but you've begun the inner conversations that start the changes.

Whenever we do spiritual work, we give off a different vibration. You might feel it in a yoga class, when you're calmer and emit less vibrational static. People like intuitive healers can feel that energetics. They follow the threads of function and dysfunction, moving energy around, out, and through, trying to create greater alignment.

This process we're sharing is a path towards better alignment. Not the way a chiropractor talks about it, but perhaps the way an orchestra conductor might. They use musical bridges to tie together different sections within a larger piece, the way you transition between different phases of your life. Feel the rhythms of your life as if you could see it as sheet music. Each of your energies, chakras, or whatever organizing system you think in, is like a line of instrumentation, like the notes for the strings, woodwinds, horns, or percussion. When you're in alignment, it all sounds beautiful. That's what we're aiming for. But there are almost certainly places where things are out of kilter, where your desires, habits, entanglements, and simple realities clash even to the point of cacophony. That can happen even if you've been trying hard to get things right, and thought you'd been making incredible progress. A jolt of change can make an even bigger sound like the clash of a cymbal or the boom of a giant drum at the end of a symphony. It may shift how people relate to you, how you relate to them, and almost certainly how you relate to yourself.

It's important to remember that the boundaries you've set up to prevent other people from seeing your struggles can prevent them from knowing what you're going through or what you need. When you stumble badly, it can sound like a musician inappropriately lurching into a strange solo. It works in jazz, where players often trade off the lead, but not so much in other styles, especially if it comes at an inopportune time. In human terms, it happens when you act out in silly or damaging ways, with an unthinking remark or an action that has harmful consequences, for yourself or others. Even if they were unintended, they can be messy, especially if you suddenly erupt after letting things fester for too long, or your response in the moment seems glaringly disproportionate to the situation.

Noisy and embarrassing, yes, but always bad? No. We're aiming for change, though preferably without negative side effects. We want all parts of you as awake as they can be. The harmony we long for takes lots of practice and probably occasional apologies along the way to your friends and neighbors, or whoever in your life has to witness the noise and flailing. But the more we wake up, the better even our practice will sound. In the meantime, while you're journaling, it's just you and your inner voice; no one else can hear you or judge you. So clash, bang, and wail away as you need to, until you feel clearer and more balanced.

Go back to the *What do you really want?* question again and again, over a cup of something hot or a shot of something tasty. Each time look for what's shifted in you, what feels different and better, and what you still need to shed or confront. Do not, I repeat do not, expect to understand it all before you say *Yes*. Trying for that is a recipe for failure and an excuse to delay. Though so is leaping without focus and intention. Much of what we are doing here is strengthening our intuition. It's time to start trusting yourself more.

Don't go racing off quickly if you're upset or frustrated. Better to take a little time to let things settle. Find your footing, even if that sometimes involves chocolate, wine, weed, shopping, or an hour or two playing your favorite game. The small bad habits will get you through the angsty places. The truly bad ones will change from doing this work. My personal preference is regular periods of epicurean silence; they invite the essence of things to make itself seen and felt. But whenever you're in doubt, follow your heart.

In time you'll find the answers you need in the language that makes the most sense to you. Your tastiest flavor will become anticipating new joys entering your life, beating out bacon, beer, or brownies, as hard as that might be to believe now. I hope that frisson of energy that change brings with it has become inviting and attractive, instead of scary, and that you look forward to the release that follows.

Whenever you feel something start to shift in you, stop and be with that. Crack your heart open. Laugh, cry, or thrash however you're moved. Now I prefer pen and paper, but in unhappy years I longed to smash crockery. You may want to rock out with dancing, heavy exercise, a blast of housework, or making a collage. Do whatever tunes you in to your bigger story. Go where the bridge is leading you.

One teacher in my Kabbalistic lineage is Colette Aboulker-Muscat, a healer and mystic in North Africa and Israel who developed powerful visualization techniques. Many use a specific breathing technique followed by quick insights with which your inner voice will prompt you. Google for books by her and her students that offer many exercises like this one. They help with all manner of changes.

Get comfy in a chair and breathe in through the nose and out through the mouth three times. Then imagine you're about to cross a narrow bridge suspended over a deep chasm. Be really visual with this. Feel the bridge swaying and the fierce winds coming at you. See the deep fast water rushing below. Feel yourself take the first step and each one after, with your hands gripping the rope rails tightly for balance. As you get to the center a monster will rise up from the depths to try and grab you. More monsters will stand watching and waiting. Feel yourself move past them. Then see your worst fear manifest to block your path. Look at it directly, even fiercely. Then walk through it to cross to the other side.

Repeat this visualization as often as you need to. Change the imagery to whatever helps you cross. Really see and feel yourself doing this. Feel the ground on the other side firm and solid beneath your feet. Feel the excitement of not falling or being captured by the monster. Feel the joy of winning what you most want. Feel how proud you are of yourself.

SECTION 4

LEARNING TO FLY

The universe buries strange jewels deep within us all, and then stands back to see if we can find them.
—ELIZABETH GILBERT

Anything that matters is here. Anything that will continue to matter in the next several thousand years will continue to be here. Approaching in the distance is the child you were some years ago. See her laughing as she chases a white butterfly.
—JOY HARJO

THE OTHER SIDE

O ne of my favorite books is very small: *Secrets from the Center of the World*. I've shared it often. Photos of the Arizona desert, each accompanied by a poem from Joy Harjo, beautiful in their nuance and subtlety, invitational in the way of a slow, deep inhalation. There is nowhere to go but into the landscape. You become as vast as sky and as small as a pebble. In the majestic stillness the poetry enters you and rests in your bones.

I used to visit a southwest dreamscape that appeared occasionally in my shamanic meditations. I could see I was headed towards far-off mountains. At first I saw myself moving from very far away. I was just a little speck, though I was very identified with that speck's progress across a rock-strewn plain. Years later, I saw myself standing at the foot of the far mesa. That meant a climb ahead and more unknowns. But I'd gotten somewhere in all the time I had been doing my inner work. A rightness fell into place with a deep knowing, a feeling like no other.

I hope you've made some similar shifts since we've met, and are beginning to feel how you're changing. Those moments are precious; they deserve gratitude. Ironically, I don't expect them often. I appreciate them all the more when they are sudden and exquisitely sweet in their all-encompassing joy. Why ice cream should be a treat not a food group.

Many years ago I studied a form of bodywork that took a while for me to loosen up and surrender to. Several months in, as an exercise in trusting my body differently, the teacher invited me to go on a blindfolded walk. It was a steep slope, or so it seemed, winding upwards through scrubby brush and then forest, on a quasi-trail used mostly by locals. Without sight, I had to rely on her completely. My spirit guides were there, but I had not yet started asking for their help in tricky circumstances. Clothing made me feel dense and heavy; it was like *klipot*, those unwanted coatings between me and the world. Once I relaxed and decided I wasn't going to fall or get hurt, I wanted to look directly from inside my soul, although I'm sure I gripped my teacher's hand so tightly that the path to my third eye was bent sideways.

She took off my blindfold when we reached the hilltop. We were not on the edge of a precipice, as I had feared, but instead in a small, inviting meadow: enough room to stretch, twirl, and revel in the freedom of unrestricted movement. I saw a green valley below, stretching wide and far. Across the way was another set of hills, close enough to seem near, but part of a future journey. I saw a magnificent raptor cruising the dappled skies and part of me flew to meet it. That image became a way to get new perspective, to see the landscape and the road in an entirely different way.

We are shown what we need to see, in ways that open us as we need to be opened. If we're lucky and paying attention, not only does the message get pinned into our consciousness, but we grok its importance. We take it in, and move forward more clearly, making progress easier and sooner. I call such times of insight *being on time in time*. They are great gifts.

Sometimes the imagery becomes iconic. One of mine came when I taught a night course at the local community college. Walking from my car, I passed a fly-fishing class. Twenty students casting in perfect unison far across a wide lawn, their lines a gorgeous arc of filament in the autumn evening, framed by birds flying south and the slowly sinking sun.

That's how I think about change. We cast our lines far into the future, aiming for something without knowing what we will catch or when. All of us striving and hoping, trusting the winds and current to carry our hopes far into the karmic waters. We have vision and desire but cannot know with certainty what will happen. Our job is to cast our lines sure and true, and then to do our work, hoping our efforts will draw the outcomes we want.

The best days are when we feel hopeful and expansive, in tune with our lives and growth. When we have been granted access, vision, and strength. When we can feel our place in the cycles of this world. I now know the way to those places and how to use them to move forward to the next and next of them. I hope you know or find yours. They are gateways that can inspire you and help compensate for some of the tough and tedious times.

I wrote this book in 2017-18, though glimmers appeared earlier. I let it grow slowly, the way I've learned gardening works best: when you're patient enough to let plants establish good roots. This can take years, but you're rewarded later by their vigor. The other side feels like that, with your roots planted firmly in self-knowing. When you realize that what you'd thought of as great effort, or perhaps even *Why do I bother?* is really, finally, clearly happening.

The last part may have felt effortless and magical. *Pop, splash, satori* you have arrived! Or maybe you kept hitting patches of scree or had to claw your way up by your fingernails. But that's behind you. Something's new and that something's you. This you is sure she doesn't want to return to how she was. You feel clear and determined. You'll resist any effort to be dragged backwards. When I felt this in a deep way, I journalled, "You made it! And you did it in your unique Helen way. You know how you've changed and effing-A you're finally letting yourself feel it." Of course, in my Helen way, I also looked around to be sure no vengeful god was listening and quickly said my prayers.

The other side always seemed so far away. We had hope, but, like the acolyte who had to reassemble herself before dawn, we were unsure if we could do what was being asked. Whether you're the planning type or the sort who jumps in without any to-do list, most of us scan the horizon when we begin a journey, whether it's a day hike or a pilgrimage. The other side doesn't seem to get closer for a long time, even with large applications of magical thinking and chocolate. Sometimes we temporarily forget about our goal because we're so engaged with what happens along the way. We enjoy prancing in front of the mirror in our workout duds, admiring our emerging muscles, and proudly grinning back at our reflection. We practice our new skills: learning to say no to the dessert platter or to an invitation from someone we're sure isn't compatible. We have more confidence, even a little moxie. If we do screw up, we bounce back faster than we used to. Then, when we look up again, we're closer to where we were headed.

In his brilliant novel *Exit West*, Mohsin Hamid uses magical realism to finesse the transition of refugees from a brutal civil war to resettlement in the West. He bypasses details of boats and borders with "doors" and poof they are there. Now what?

That first footstep on the other side is different. I'm a sucker for the teasing glimpses but this is a visceral shift. All your senses are lined up and firing in synch. You're a different version of you and you can feel it, from the moment you wake up and throughout your day. That's what the other side feels like, even if the feeling doesn't last. You're not deluded; you realize you'll have to make more journeys. But not now. Now you get to feel how grand it is to stand on the top of that small mountain, see behind what you've traversed, and trust tomorrow's trek will be easier.

To be clear: there is no literal other side to this incarnation except death, and only those in agony choose that transition. For most of us the struggles are more manageable. We're still living our messy humanness, but now we have the tools and know that we can succeed. We've been tested by life and we have tested ourselves. We know we can become stronger and more whole. We've signed up to keep learning, to stay vulnerable, and to keep growing. But we've begun to welcome that choice, not fear it.

That knowledge is what gives you energy. When you realize that the you you'd hoped to become is starting to feel like a you that suits you. You like whom you see in the mirror. She smiles back with confidence, and the occasional saucy grin. She gives you a fresher perspective. You can look forward to what's coming next and after, because each other side is a door you're ready to walk through.

It's time to pack your satchel again. Not like a refugee but with foresight and intention. You have the luxury of choosing with your heart, not out of necessity. The hounds are long behind you; no one is chasing. You can pack for a picnic, putting in big words like freedom and choice, strength, and trust in yourself. Those are the moments I love the best.

Do you feel a shift? Does it feel real? Give you more confidence? Inspire you?

Can you hear yourself telling the story of your transition?

Now that you're on the other side, what other parts of your story do you want to change?

What're you most afraid you will need to face and do?

What is the smallest step you could take in that direction?

Are you ready to do that now? If not, how can you prepare?

What, Me Worry?

When I was a kid, the closest thing to satire like *The Onion* or *Saturday Night Live* was *Mad* magazine, with the wildly grinning Alfred E. Newman beaming from every cover: a crazy, wise fool cast as a broad-eared, freckled redhead, his Mona Lisa grin saying he gets the joke and it's on you. His tagline was "What, me worry?"

Most of us don't get that kind of easy pass. Our lives are filled 24/7 with family, work, health, and money, to name just some biggies. We juggle all the daily concerns, thinking our plates are full and overfull. Then the phone rings, or the doctor speaks, and our lives are upended by jolts of drama. Anxious, future-tripping, scenario-spinning us's grab the helm, living all the possible what-ifs we can conjure. Rarely in those circumstances does our imagination offer us anything happy or good. Hours and energy spent scaring ourselves with all the bad things that might possibly happen. Then we make our vows, bargaining with whomever or whatever we pray to. As backup we try on our heroics, because we want them on tap, even if our capes are a little dusty or tattered. And we test out our rhetoric in imaginary conversations, all the while looking around for the exits, less sure of ourselves than we should be.

What's the old adage? "Ninety percent of what you worry about never happens." But we keep fretting about what we need to do more or less of, tantalized and frustrated by success that hasn't yet manifested but we still want and can almost taste. Often we hope for great results overnight, which I used to call my Wake Up Thin Fantasy. We fantasize that the problem will *poof!* go away or that we'll be rescued from our responsibility for dealing with it. Magical thinking can improve your mood, but it's not quite the same as tackling what you need to. A favorite quote, seen recently as graffiti: "Worry is a terrible waste of imagination." Yes! Instead of fretting, use your imagination for making love or beauty, or for finding the right allies to help you.

Instead of fearing the future, become more open, even curious. Don't be shy about talking about what you're afraid of. Whatever your right-now lessons are, the people around you are there for a reason, and part of that reason is to help. That's obvious for your friends and family, the ones with whom you're hand-in-hand; but it's true too for your nemesis or those that throw you off-kilter. All of them can help you find answers, or at least give you clues. One thing to watch out for: most of us shift how we discuss what's bothering us depending on whose ear the story is falling into. We shade the nuances of the story, shifting responsibility and blame to make ourselves look less culpable, even if we end up looking a little like victims. Sympathy feels better than shame, even if we're shoveling shame, blame, guilt, and more down our own gullets.

A cautionary note: When you tell a story about your troubles, don't be surprised if what comes back at you shifts your basic assumptions. Most people are smart enough to pick through the half-truths and ask you the tough questions. If they're not, expand your circle. Listen even—or perhaps especially—if it's what you most don't want to hear. You don't have to buy anyone else's take like it's gospel, but you do need to consider their insights, because you can't see their perspective from the middle of your own story. Sometimes their savvy and questions will be exactly what your inner voice has been shouting at you, though you may have that channel turned down too low to hear it.

Even with help on tap, we often feel alone in the dark when we're wrestling our tough stuff. About a decade ago, I made a commitment to a three-year spiritual initiation. Then I went about enjoying my life without doing anything much differently. Three months in I was on a hike and tripped on a root, or perhaps on nothing at all. As I fell I promised, *I'll do my work, I swear. No crises, no crises, no crises, please no crises!* I was horrified to think I'd screwed up so quickly simply by doing nothing, a good reminder that when we finally do make a commitment there are consequences for failing to follow through. On the ground, I slowly checked for broken limbs or smashed glasses and repeated my vow. When I made it home I called my friend the intuitive and asked, "Is it always this lonely?," and she said, "No." Eventually that became true, in part because of my relationship with the spirit guides who'd invited me to walk that path.

I once heard a story about how the spiritual journey unfolds in metaphorical time. Day One was believing in things like acupuncture and Reiki. Day Two, reincarnation and multiple interacting worlds. Day Three, turning around to see a holographic-looking guide in your 3-D reality. I'm mostly a Day Two kinda gal. I care more about style than physical manifestation, which might scare the poop right out of me. I want spirit guides accessible and benevolent, timely and truthful, candid and clear, especially about touchy subjects. An occasional flash of humor is reassuring, like finding the answer to yesterday's doubts right next to the keys I'm frantically searching for.

Guides may be completely imaginary, a clever fabrication of some needy part of my psyche. Some people put them in the same category as believing angels or imaginary friends for three-year olds. Fine for them. I treat guides like a mirror that's wiser and at least a few steps ahead of my 24/7 self. They come when you're ready to listen; no eBay or Amazon link will fetch them. You need to invite, not pursue. As any unrequited lover has learned: needy ain't sexy. But whether you say intuition, God, guide, angels, Jesus, or no words at all, if you open to the world of the unseen, you'll have as much access as you're ready for.

Mostly guides are generous with information and suggestions. Like your besties, guides want you to avoid life's hassles. But there are lots of unfinished conversations, because they're mentors, not fix-alls. Mine are DIYers, as in *You already know the answer. Please do what we've been telling you (for so long)*. Unless it's a life-threatening crisis, the instructions are rarely direct. But when you find yourself journaling or thinking the same things over and over, you're generally on the right track to making some progress. I'll confess up front that, at least for me, saying and doing are very different levels of commitment. In my life there's a whole lot of saying, and repeating, and questioning, and saying again, and repeating some more that precedes what might not look like a whole lot of doing. But once I finally get my butt into gear, I can see how the small doings have added up over time, and how all the questioning and refining has prepped me for bigger doings.

When you're truly ready for change, all your wishing and hoping and praying really does move things along, if only because you're probably sick of your own pacing in front of the doorway to change.

In your longing for rescue, be careful about trusting any energy that appears. Remember, luck comes in two flavors. Every culture honors trickster guides: Coyote, Loki, Fox, Monkey, Chango, Anansi, and Hermes. They're almost always the gods of magic and secrets as well as of healing. Trickster guides delight in your foibles. It takes work to know them, but they're important teachers, carriers of crazy wisdom that shakes things up and opens huge new options in a flash. Their road is filled with surprises, plus unexpected blessings and hidden pitfalls. It can feel like a giant carnival ride, scary fun that leaves you exhausted and yet somehow ready to do it again. As Neil Gaiman writes: "Loki makes the world more interesting but less safe. You resent him even when you're most grateful, and you're grateful to him even when you hate him the most." How often have you trusted someone like that, realizing your folly only too late?

With guides you can share your fears and hopes without feeling any sillier than a three-year-old at a tea party. Suspending disbelief magnifies your intuition geometrically. If you're willing to flex your belief muscles, ask your own guides to visit as you do this work, whether you have iconography or confidence in them or not. That's it. Nothing more complicated. If something seems to happen, notice how you feel when it does. Like any new art form, this takes practice, but it doesn't respond well to demands. Invite help; ask for help; give thanks for help; and pay attention to how it arrives and what it is telling you.

Guidance means literally that: a nod in the right direction. You still need to do the work.

What spirit wants to tell you is just a nanosecond a way. Just an iota of space and time between being in pain and clueless to having new insight and direction. Being unconscious can last lifetimes, if you're not paying attention or unwilling to take in what you hear. For me, not much beats believing that my inner voice just got a massive text alert from energies that are my guides and cheerleaders. When I listen and respond, things always improve.

You've probably learned the hard way that whining or failing to really show up is often rewarded with another dose of the same lesson. If you don't hear or heed early warning signals, the ante gets upped, often at an especially inconvenient time. A car accident when you're running late for your interview, the worst date ever while you're recovering from a bad breakup, screwing up a big project at work right before evaluation and bonus time, to name just a few. The bigger jolts cost time, energy, and self-confidence, even anguish. Instead, cultivate a gut rightness about what to do next. Then follow up by doing what you've been told to change; short-circuit the whining and fretting, and then set your path. You get more oomph and an extra dose of sixth sense. It might sometimes hit like a triple latte, but it almost always ends the thrashing and moaning and replaces it with a simple clarity that can become a reliable guide.

When I play cards I say luck is my favorite suit. But luck favors those who court her. When I wrote to a friend, "I'm ready for whatever the Universe sends," I realized I'd finally healed something deep and essential. Maybe I'm a late bloomer. For me, unplugging from fear was a huge step. Folks with a lifetime of feeling responsible and robust worry genes think using them is what keeps the universe running on its rails. Lololololol. We used to be called "planners" to our faces and "control freaks" *sotto voce.* Learning to trust is hard, and life's daily lessons don't always encourage it as a reliable habit. But trust is a prerequisite to virtually all the lessons that we encounter.

Sometimes caution's a good thing. When your world's filled with sabertooths, a sharp spear and sharper hearing makes a lots of sense. Twenty-first century lessons are less life-threatening but still important: lock your doors, change your passwords, and figure out how to discern truth from all the noisy fakery. The worry and pacing, not so useful. Staying present helps us see how what's looming impacts our plans, let alone our imminent safety. That assumes we're clear-headed and far-sighted, another good reason to stick with your *Yes.* We can hope we're blessed or lucky, and that what's coming towards us doesn't hurt, with bonus points for packaging and timing. There's lots I'd do to avoid a broken leg or flat tire, let alone something far more serious. But we don't often get a choice. Most days we do the best we can, in a shoulder shrugging coulda, shoulda, woulda done better kind of way. But when you're really in the heart of it, in that moment when you can't afford to screw up or you may never try again, pull every trick out of your toolkit, and use every ounce of courage and faith in yourself to do your very, very best.

A friend was taking a big, entrepreneurial leap with many options ahead, from success and glory to *Yikes! What if I lose my house?* She told me she'd taken to watching *Naked and Afraid,* and said the first thing most folks did was to cover themselves with mud. It helps prevent insect bites and made them feel less vulnerable. As their obstacles unfolded, most were reduced from eating berries to eating bugs, and, ugh, her worst: scorpions. She said, "As long as I'm not eating scorpions, I can think it's all gonna be okay."

If your life's at that kind of edge, absolutely plan to minimize damage. Do it with help from folks who know you, who understand what you're facing, and who have useful skills. Develop exit strategies, emotional through financial, and plan for lousy, expensive failures as well as joyous wins. Balance them as best you can. Pay extra close attention if you find yourself daydreaming or thinking about only one or the other end of the spectrum.

Healthy portions of worry are legit in a crisis or a huge life experiment. But the lower level fretting just isn't worth it. Scared your special so-and-so doesn't care enough? Send a sweet note. Afraid your fancy pants don't fit? Lose five pounds. A problem at work? Call a meeting. Much of what we waste time worrying about belongs in the don't-sweat-the-small-stuff bin and can be easily altered by quick, common sense interventions.

Time is precious. Stop wasting it on worry. Instead, in the time you liberate, do something good for yourself. Go hang with a friend, preferably a happy one. Grab a great book, movie, or recipe. Change your playlist. Do something silly. As a crazy, wise friend once told me, "Run around the room with your underwear on your head and yell "I can do this!" really, really loud!" I never did. But I sort of wish I had.

Find a comfy, quiet place and ten minutes where you can ignore people and your phone. Set a timer so you don't wonder if it's been one minute or three hours. Think about something that's been absorbing too much time on your mental channels. Don't be shy about choosing a gnarly story you keep feeling stuck in, especially one that feels ultra tough: one with no good end in sight, let alone one you'd embrace.

Then let 'er rip. Feel your frustration, anger, helplessness, confusion, and just plain pissy-ness, plus all your fears about how your history impacts your future before imagining better endings to this story. Hang in there the whole time, even if your mind wanders to shopping lists or your honey or your lack of one.

Even if you think it's hooey, invite your guides to chime in. Listen for a new voice. Maybe you'll hear nothing at all. No matter what, you've opened a door. See who comes knocking. Maybe not today, but soon.

Try this more often than you feel like you need to.

ONE MORE TIME

The Jewish year is divided into two halves. Rosh Hashanah, the official new year, starts in autumn, before the time of growing dark and going inward, just as Jewish days begin at sundown, the time before night and dreaming. The rituals for the ten-day High Holidays that Rosh Hashanah begins are about starting over, about forgiving yourself and others for the sins of the past, and promising to do better going forward. It's not unlike what many folks do on January 1, but in Jewish rituals we atone for various "sins" in the collective identity (e.g. "We have slandered, we have lied, we have stolen"), as opposed to a single penitent voice saying, "I screwed up."

The second half of the year begins in spring, in the first calendar month (yes, it's a contradiction), with Passover, the holiday of remembering the exodus from Egypt, the place of constriction. It's when we're asked to look deeply at how we still limit ourselves, and reaffirm our desire to be free, even if that will mean a difficult liberation process that includes embracing a scary unknown. If we do not take this risk, we remain slaves to our resistance to change.

One thing I truly value about Judaism is that the annual calendar is organized around a spiritual framework of rituals like this. I'm not very observant in practice. But where soul and life cohabit in that kind of harmony, I have a deeply reverent heart.

Reality checks are good to do regularly. I give myself a report card, sector by sector of my life: from relationship with food to how I spend my time. The kind we got in grammar school, or did in the days before everyone got an *A* for participating. Tell yourself what you're proud of, but also be honest about where you're slacking. These check-ins are not just to make you face the scale the next morning, but rather to support your intention to change. In a typical year, every three or four months for a serious report card can help you build up enthusiasm. But when you're feeling like it really matters to have more accountability—do it much more often. Most of us backslide too often in the beginning. But then we get back to work. One *Yes* is never enough.

For as impatient and quick as I often am, I genuinely believe in process. In time. In the importance of actually doing your work, not just talking about it. Folks who know me will attest to my ability to procrastinate. But once I finally settle into doing, even with occasional loop-de-loop rounds, my doings begin to become habit, and supplant the old behaviors, that last twenty pounds notwithstanding. From the outside, the process looks like spaghetti; linear progress has very little home in this part of my universe. But even though I've failed spectacularly and often, I've also learned that all the worst failure does is create momentary shame, and eventually that too will turn into motivation, however slow or belated.

When you get a *C* on your report card, you'll probably feel like you failed. No biggie. Unpacking how you did helps you "hit the reset button," a phrase I use often. It implies a do-over that might vault you past the next starting line, maybe with extra credit for prior earnestness. Every time we begin again we go through all the stages, from high hopes to hard work. *Damn, it's back to go. Why couldn't this be easy and done already?* Because changing isn't. Start over in steps small enough to succeed; let those lead to bigger ones, even if you don't always see what's in front of your nose.

One good indicator that you need to do more is when you walk around hearing "It's not fair!" ringing in your head. Even after a big shift, most of us develop new, self-serving scripts of all the ways that we've changed and our commensurate expectations about how the universe should be responding and treating us, as in so much better than it seems to be doing. We're resentful that we haven't gotten the rewards we think we deserve, and wonder if all the effort was worth it, if it's always going to feel so much harder than we expected it to be. Translation: No, you're not done yet.

To be clear, not changing wouldn't have been easy either. Because you weren't happy, knew you weren't happy, and knew you had to choose some kind of *Yes*, even if you couldn't give it a shape or name. Good news: you get as many chances to figure this out as you get breaths and nows. You can say *Yes* again any time you're ready. Or you can go buy a bigger, stretchier size, and say it later. Honestly, no one cares about this more than you. Your mother, spouse, therapist, or friends all have opinions, and will likely share them whether you ask them or not. But the one to whom success matters most is you. And the one who has to make it stick is also you.

Often we repeat *Yes* out of duty or like it's a punishment. After you say *Yes, I'm in for another round*, I hope you can find the joy in it. As one of my besties says, "Never start a diet unless you're excited about it." Beyond the work, remember you have heady jolts of success and pride in your future. That's not a quick hit of joy like a piece of birthday cake. But when folks start to notice that you're happier and more successful with your issues, you'll puff up with pride about how happy you are being your new you, and how much you like living her.

I've skied only once and resisted the instruction, "Sit lower and you'll go faster." I do not go bungee jumping or paragliding. My risk tolerance is low. But this I believe with all my heart: the joy you can get from this kind of progress is as fabulously wonderful as what snowboarders or ski jumpers must feel when they untether from the earth. During the last Olympics I felt ready for another round with my sugar demon. I placed a sign on the fridge: "If they can do that, I can do this." That small but potent reminder, strategically located, reinforced better choices until they happened most of the time. Whatever you can say that you'll listen to, post it where you'll see it. Not to shame yourself but to keep your goals in sight.

Here's a lesson I learned when a friend worked in an art gallery: Her boss invited me to make a box out of plexiglass remnants, a careful process of cutting, sanding, gluing, and lots of waiting. Just before the glue had finally set, he carefully inspected my efforts, saying "Looks great." And then, to my horror, he slowly tore it into pieces. "Now you know you can do it," he said, "so do it again. And do it better."

That's what this messy joys concept is all about. If we'd already gotten our attempts to change right, we'd all be angels or enlightened enough not to worry about our pants size, or what we choose to do with our time, money, or attentions. Instead, we come in this life to do karma cleaning. We write all our complicated and engaging human dramas to keep ourselves engaged and entertained while we do our soul work.

I hope you like starring in your story. It's harder and sad when we don't. The price we pay, the ante, is doing our work, with all our charms and foibles, and all our ways to get it wrong. But the most wonderful and perhaps important thing about us is this: we keep trying. And somehow, through accident, intuition, or sheer hard work, we start to do better. We clean up our act and our karma. We choose the salad more often than the fries. We become kinder, more generous, softer, and more caring. We choose better sooner and more often.

Jews more religious than I am eat only kosher foods, which means forswearing shellfish and pork among other rules. But the basic concept of defined limits, this is allowed and this is not, is especially useful when you're trying to say another *Yes*. Because some habits, people or situations are simply toxic for us. When we're around them we slip into patterns we thought we'd left far behind. We see ourselves acting in ways we hoped we were long passed. We hear ourselves saying things we thought we'd never hear again, and realize we're feeling emotions like shame and a vague (or stronger) sense of anxiety. When you're having that kind of flashback, pay very close attention. If you need a shot of courage, remember the #metoo movement, and the long line of courageous young gymnasts looking their abuser in the eye. You'll realize that there's no part of you cannot reclaim. Brief exposures to toxic folks or situations won't kill you.

They're actually a pretty good litmus test of your progress. But if you feel yourself feeling weaker, diminished, tentative, or less happy than you've been, pay extra careful attention.

For long periods of my life I put everyone's needs ahead of mine: partner, boss, friends, whoever needed me most right then. I developed bad patterns with people who I wanted to love me or whose neediness seemed more urgent than my own priorities. Work was often the high bidder, but the heart gave it a good run. I was more unconscious than I realized, so true change was stalled at the gate. When your head is full of other folks' stories, it's too easy to divert yourself from what you should do for yourself. Putting yourself into their story is always a tempting distraction, because you can play the hero or otherwise avoid what you'd rather not face. But when your issues are center stage, you have to show up, and remember that you matter too.

If you like historical thrillers, read Alan Furst's novels of World War II Europe 1939–1943, a time before the winning outcome was clear. Every character faces difficult choices amid fear and very real danger. Values take on new weight when your life is on the line. People don't always choose self-interest, but they have to decide very clearly, and sometimes quickly, what matters most. In your life the stakes may sometimes feel like that, but I hope they're not life and death very often.

When you're eyeball-to-eyeball with your crap, and you need perspective, ask your best friend. She'll help you remember how far you've come: how you've been hurt, the battles you fought, the ones you lost and the ones you won. Let her be your map for a while, or help you smooth out the creases and interpret the spots that have become hard to read. It may cost some pride and laughter to have your stubborn recidivism at the center of the bulls-eye. But it'll help you flip past what Anne Lamott describes as "how we make important changes—barely, poorly, slowly."

When your issues cycle around look at them unafraid. Your transition is already underway. The biggest *Yes* is behind you. A thousand smaller ones may lie ahead. But now we are insulated and buoyed by hope. We have more courage. Change may be intermittent, like spotty cell coverage, but we're more fit, more curious, and even a little frisky. We're not looking for danger, but we're confident we'd do better in a jam. We're learning how to bounce, and that it's okay to shake things up. Pushing ourselves feels better, even a little fun, like *Look Ma, no hands!*

Everyone's got a siren we feel helpless to resist, despite every vow and good intention. If you don't know what I'm talking about, your DNA's not fully human. Mine's been food. You know yours. They may start as self-soothing but have grown into habits that define and limit us. We push and we try, but until we clear out the root causes, change can be as many steps back as we have taken forward. Changing yourself at a core level is a long path.

Be proud of yourself for however far you get each time you try.

There's not much better on a crisp October night than a haunted corn maze. Ours has silly puzzles to solve; the answers tell you to go right or left so you make it out before closing. Turn a corner to find escaped mental patients, alien abductors, or evil clowns with chainsaws. If you don't pee yourself laughing, or trip trying to push a friend into their path instead of you, it's cathartic for the soul. Also, you know they'll eventually let you out. But when it's your life, and you can't be sure of rescue, you have to get the answers right to make it home.

We do this dance times beyond counting. But eventually, miraculously, something shifts. With my issues what changed was inner. Sure, I'd learned a lot in diet and health programs. But when I did this work, something shifted in my foundations. Like a house finally settled into bedrock, I realized I'd been liking myself much better for a very long time. It had little to do with what I weighed and lots to do with being happier. Then the changes got easier, even easy. I rarely ignore a plate of brownies, but I've learned to pause, and how to say "No, thanks" or enjoy just one, actually tasting it instead of waking up from a last bite I can barely remember.

An elegant *Downton Abbey* star plays a con artist in a new series. She surrounds herself with affirmation-spouting self-help tapes; but they turn into white noise as she lights another cigarette or preps her next high. The *do it right* words are part her story, but not yet inside her until, many mistakes later, she's finally ready.

There comes a moment when you realize your growth has been exponential. That you're getting it right more often and more quickly. Instead of three tries it takes one, or even none. You make the right choice more easily and without a lot of fuss. It's not a linear process and it's not reliable for a long while, but starting to trust yourself more is a very cool feeling.

The next round will be different. You won't get suckered by cheap bait or distract yourself. You'll care more, be more patient, and be steady on as you go. You won't shake up your life out of escapism or boredom. Sure, you may have a sundae or a self-indulgent weekend. But you won't do it all the time.

Serious note: If you do indulge, please enjoy it! Enjoy every bite and every moment without giving yourself a hard time. Unless your life is on the line (and for some it might be) it's the guilt that's deadly, not the occasional lapse. Let yourself feel good about your choices because you've earned them. You'll stay on track more because you've started believing the new and better stories that you've been telling yourself. Much of this work is about trusting your own word. Not just saying those words but feeling them in your bones. It's you hitting the reset button.

Two of the most important practices in my life have come from two very different versions of a gift. First, at the end of the brief but timely relationship I was gifted a small journal. Sounds nice, but it was clearly a re-gift, a leatherette pad that might've cost a dime in a dollar store. I used it for the burning ritual (where you write down whatever you're done with, burn the pages, and then toss the ashes).

The second came decades later, from a dear friend. I use it for a ritual I call "The 10 Commandments." Not now-to-eternity commandments, but a game plan for the next week or a month. You can do it after a report card or spontaneously. With health for example, they might include: limits on sugar, carbs, or calories; learning portions; or exercise goals. For money: limits on spending in various categories or mandatory savings. For a relationship: compromises on thorny issues that cause tension or poor communication, from capping the toothpaste to better listening. I include my primary commandment: Breathe and remember the pause button.

Whatever your issue, think about how you feel when you get it right, and how you feel when you've blown it. Think about what triggers screwing up. Then imagine some simple ritual you could do instead, or at least before, like having a cup of tea. Forgive yourself if you blow it again. But keep asking and feeling for a shift.

FEEDING MYSELF TIME

Amazingly, fantastically, delightfully there comes a moment when you realize you've made progress. When you look for yourself in the mirror and realize that you're much closer to the you that you've been aiming for.

For me, that took a long time. I spent decades practicing yo-yo dieting, though the periods of over-eating and bemoaning my midriff were many and the dieting happened in briefer stints, never to goal. But as a story it took up a lot of space in my life. Why my friends roll their eyes each time I say, "It's time to get on program again." Your journey, whether it's food, money, drugs, relationship, or some other ongoing battle, probably looks the same. I use the food metaphor because it's the one I've lived, but please sub your own patterns in as you read. The symptoms and cures are pretty much the same, unless you're dealing with hard drugs or bankruptcy, which are out of my league.

As I walked through my kitchen I saw a note to self: "It's time to become a renunciate again." It was déjà vu all over again, as the saying goes. In me, the blend between renunciation and self-indulgence looks like a lava lamp: one part always dialed to the contemplative channel, the other wondering what's for dinner. They intermingle with a bemused curiosity, but they're cautious sisters, not best friends; they never quite grok the other's why, like a first date that leaves you feeling something important is missing, even if you can't quite name it.

I move freely between both ends of any span. I'm social and reclusive, generous and selfish, insightful and obtuse, productive and lazy, plus a zillion others in sometimes fascinating combinations. As Daniel Mendelsohn so eloquently deconstructs in *The Elusive Embrace*, "We're always two things at once."

Whatever I'm being, I feel fully that, at least for the moment. But at some point in every dimensional field the pendulum swings. We do it ourselves or the gods and fates do it for us. At the tightest stretch of my yoga pants, I need a swift kick, which I appear structurally unable to administer. If what faces me is painful, or if I'm feeling rebellious, I'll drag my heels and mutter, "No, no, no," for seemingly effing forever, even knowing it's long past time to get moving. Even at my seemingly obedient best, I'm secretly looking for escape hatches. Surrender comes hard, but the price of not surrendering is higher, like my lost years. Until we learn acceptance, we often pace like a fox in a trap, unknowing of what will come but reflexively and fiercely resistant to change in all but our words.

People learning about meditation often talk about "monkey mind." That's when you're thinking about everything except nothing: grocery lists, an overdue memo, your bank account or schedule, anything except simply your breath. For most of us the airwaves are crowded, and our inner scripts are in heavy rotation, but amazingly, if we remember to stop and listen, we have access to the highest wisdom. There's lots to learn from chaos, but the static and frenzy keeps us from integrating. In the silence, be it mediation, prayer, or staring at nature, we learn to slow down. The dross falls away and we can really hear what we're being told. As those messages seep in, the yearning for more softness and more stillness keeps calling to us.

In an earlier part of my life, when I had a job, I struggled with binging on sugar. Sugar is highly reliable, easily obtainable, and immediately gratifying. In my life, there's always been a too-small gap between cookie commercials and opening the cupboards. My whopping big excuse: a quick flash of pleasure before someone came knocking, needing me. But sugar destroys more than it creates, so I decided to feed myself time instead of sugar.

Retirement means no longer organizing your identity and schedule around work; it clears time to try watercolors or learn to play the piano. So in a world where anything is possible, what happens to the need-ice-cream-now voice? It gets quieter. With less to suppress there's less to resist. Sweets can be treats, not a way to appease other hungers. And new treats like fresh fruits and veggies have room to introduce themselves and become tasty alternatives. I'm convinced you can do it sooner than retirement. But that means becoming happier in your 24/7/365 world.

In all the movies, right before the battle scenes, something changes in the eyes, posture, and bearing of the characters: all focus, all in. Ironically, feeding yourself time is the opposite of that. Instead of a blade's edge between life and death, it's about slowing down with the expansive sense of *hamakom*: all the freedom to be fully present without wrestling with questions or doubts. It's not a brain or thinking thing. It's an act of settling in, of beingness, of knowing things are mostly all right, and you can do something about the ones that aren't later. And you don't need sugar to remember that.

Even if you're working two jobs and feeding a family, fight for time for you. Think farmers markets, not microwaves. Chopping, stirring, sniffing will help your senses and feelings shift. Mark the calendar on the day you realize you're lusting for a spoonful of a new recipe instead of hungering for sugar or chips. Remember your answer to *What do you really want?* Or perhaps dream up a better one now. Keep reminding yourself what matters is having a soul purpose as well as material goals.

The first piece of time to feed yourself is the pause button. As you get used to chilling instead of scurrying, you'll realize that your biggest hungers aren't as hungry as they were, and that you've become more curious about what else you could be doing. And whether that's culling or cleaning or just making lists, it's not eating. It also gets you a bit more ready to go for a walk or to the gym. To feel how you feel in your body. To go dancing, or get sensual, and walk around with a smile on your face instead of crumbs on your shirt.

Feeding yourself time is not about measuring calories or minutes. It's feeling so present being you that you're one with what and where you are. There's no gaps around you for desire to creep in, no empty spaces to try and fill, no loneliness or boredom to stiff-arm with pretzels or popcorn. While you're getting to that lovely Zen-like space, you'll start making better choices: craving a carrot or a peach, sitting with a book instead of rummaging the cupboards for a treat. Making time to meet a friend for tea. Knowing there's nothing you cannot have, but that you don't need it right now, and that instead, you can have this moment of being fully present all the time, and that you can savor it very, very slowly.

I hope you get this feeling so much earlier than I did. Perhaps when the robots take over and a universal wage is the norm, we'll all have time to become creative dreamers. Until then, you're going to have make peace and quiet more of a priority. Maybe learn to say "No, thanks" when people ask you to do things. Perhaps make a little show of consulting your calendar app, and then saying, "I'm sorry, I have a prior commitment." The truth is you do, and that commitment is you.

Whatever it is you most hunger for, beyond the surface wants of comfort or luxury, the hardest truth about being incarnate is remembering that our time here is finite. We wear these lovely bodies that do so many wonderful, joyous things. We have such warm and generous souls. And we get to be us for only such a brief time. Somehow you have to make your peace with that, and create balance between the immediacy of joys like sugar and your answer to *What do you really want?* If you can make that sweet spot your home base you won't have to get older to be happier.

In Torah the Jews travelled through the desert for forty years, sustained by manna that they harvested each morning. Hoarding got you nowhere. If you took more than you needed for the day it spoiled. But new fresh and delicious (as in tasting like whatever you most wanted it to be) manna showed up each day to be gathered and eaten. Manna's not just a way to explain the logistics of feeding that many folks for so long. It's a metaphor about learning to trust the bounty and beneficence of the universe. To believe that you don't have to hug your plate the way folks in prison movies do, gobbing it in seconds afraid that someone hungrier and more assertive will snatch it. No one I know gets that kind of manna, but we are given so very much.

One of my regular practices is gratitude. Not just saying thanks when something good happens or after I've made it through a tough passage, but every day. I give thanks for being happy, being me, being able to do what I want, and for the simple joys of food, shelter, and safety, plus all the abundance of love in my life. When I do that, feeding myself time becomes the most glorious feast.

In Luis Alberto Urrea's marvelous novel *The House of Broken Angels,* the dying protagonist fills journal after journal with gratitude, the bittersweet legacy of knowing his time is short. It is gratitude from a life well lived and loved, spanning the smell of a sudden rainstorm to memories of his first true love. Better to give thanks every moment instead of waiting until the brink of your final transition.

For one week, take a minute each evening before dinner or bedtime to think about three good things that happened that day. See how doing just that one thing ripples through your life, and see if it helps you stay on your program, however you're defining it now.

Try doing it longer, say another week. If you slack, forgive yourself, and then agree to begin again, perhaps "next Monday" (LOL the traditional beginning of many change cycles), or "the first of next month." By all means start sooner if you're so moved. But only when you are doing it out of hope, not out of obligation.

If you have close friends or family with whom you talk about heart-based things, develop a practice of sharing your gratitudes. They can include "I love you," because we never hear that often enough. But they can also be the simple things that made your day or week kinder and sweeter. It feeds the energetics we share, and feeds our souls.

P.S. Notice if you want to share your gratitudes more often and even randomly which can surprisingly open up both new and old relationships in deeper ways. I suspect you will smile and be happy when you do.

Binge Watching

Years ago, before binge watching was a common way to consume series TV, I was horrified when a friend told me she'd spent an entire Sunday watching a full season of an HBO series. Months later, when I had to pause episode four of *Six Feet Under* to go to a dinner party, I got it. It's satisfying to peek ahead. To look at the *What happens next?* aspects of life without having to wait a week—or in real time often much longer—for the next installment: to find out if your crush is reciprocal, your application scores an interview, or all's well in the end.

We're told to be here now. Be in the moment. Take life one step at a time. Stay present. Focus. Don't worry or anticipate. Don't be a control freak. We're also told to vision and plan, to manage our lives carefully, and to be prepared. Yes, there are contradictions. But the assumption is that if you're calmer, more present, and don't respond reflexively and reactively, you'll do a better job managing your life. Hard as it may be to practice, the teachers keep telling us that one breath at a time is the right speed. One inhale and one exhale, again and again, until we are fully present. Maybe not a full *hineini* (*I am here*), but a helluva good place to start. Do that most of the time, even when you're at work, cooking, cleaning, or (yikes!) even on a date or in an argument, and you're ninety percent to where you want to go.

Would that wanting made it so. Our attention is split in several directions almost all the time: family, work, and the irresistible chirps of our screens. We get unplugged moments, but they're usually involuntary, like when you reach for your cell phone and realize you've left it behind. After the panic subsides you might even enjoy being untethered (after you take a quick inventory of what's urgent and might go wrong without you). I know folks who take one day a week offline, a cyber Shabbat, not even a peek, and they swear it's incredibly relaxing. I unplug in shorter bursts, but the principle holds. What matters most is creating space and time for simply being quiet, and doing that at least as often as you cheer for your team or do house chores. For some training reps, practice driving without responding to your phone's beeps; you'll avoid a hefty fine and the roads will be safer for the rest of us.

Sometimes it takes all your energy to slow down. We who've had insomnia practice in the wee hours, as we invite sleep to return. That's also when all our demons and dreams come knocking, the ones who make us fearful and optimistic in self-negating measure as we imagine what might happen in our ongoing dramas. Not a great formula for relaxation. Deep breathing's a far better choice.

Most of us are impatient for success. We cram everything in, afraid we'll miss a chance at what might make us happy. We live with FOMO (fear of missing out), whether it's active or subliminal. We swallow without tasting, racing towards dessert. Aim to tame that part of you. Yes, you may occasionally miss something wonderful, but short of the last ride out of a disaster zone, your life will move forward on the right track. A friend was dating a man who was perpetually broke, who couldn't resist every pretty thing, and when confronted by his empty bank account replied with, "You have to create emptiness for joy to flow into it." Raised by immigrants, I reject poverty consciousness as the basis of a safe life. But his logic was irrefutable. You need to leave open spaces for surprises to appear.

There's always something we miss out on by "doing nothing," but that nothing is the most important gift you can give your soul. If you don't know Elizabeth Gilbert's TED Talk on creativity, it is an absolute must-see. She nails the complex relationship between imagination, creativity, and the muses that inspire us. Gilbert tells a fabulous story of a poet caught walking in a field who hears some wonderful lines wafting by, but she has nothing write with, and feels them slip through her and go onto the next deserving soul. Every creative mourns such losses, but eventually we learn that new words will come knocking, and that some days being in the field is more important than capturing the poem. It's how you restore an elemental part of you. From that renewal, a new and different creativity will emerge. I hope the poet celebrated inspiration knocking at her door, because that connection nourishes the very heart of you and invites more inspiration to come visit.

Those who believe this isn't our first lifetime live with a double-edged sword. We want to get our karma as right as possible this time around. But while we hope to succeed, we implicitly assume there'll be more chances to correct our mistakes, even if we're no longer this us. This time around, we want our lessons with lotus blossoms and chocolate, not physical or emotional pain, dislocated homes or body parts, or even regular inconveniences. We want to feed on joy and success, hoping other lifetimes have taken the brunt of life's hardships. We're impatient in the hard transitions, hoping to avoid both the rocks and bumps of the journey, let alone outright failure. We'd like a cruise-control version of our karma road, replete with pretty scenery and good eateries. But we're pretty sure that won't last long, so we waste time and energy fearing what's around the bend.

Binge watching moves us past the fear. It also short-circuits our curiosity. It allows us clarity but offers less perspective. We get a speedy version, not one that stimulates our neuro-networks. Slowing down gives us time to care about the characters, get involved in their dramas, and reflect on how we might do in similar circumstances. Binge watching takes away the mystery as well as the suspense.

We twenty-first century humans are slowly (or quickly) losing our stamina to hang in with an evolving plot line. We're forgetting the benefits of resilience, of bouncing after a loss, and of how good it can feel to start again and get it right, or at least better, the next time around. Studies have shown our species has a shrinking attention span. When the Internet's on-demand in your pocket, why should you try to remember things? Answer: It's like going to the gym. If you don't use your remembering muscles, you're going to lose them. For sure they'll get flaccid and flabby.

The best of us, the wise ones and the saints, can remember lifetimes and their biggest lessons: *Learn kindness and compassion. Choose balance. Create beauty. Make love not war.* The rest of us need lots of reminders.

This perspective helps me understand why I'm becoming more of a hermit, why my muses and the gentle winds of evening are my chosen companions. I need the constraint of simplicity to keep myself on track. I need to hear what the silence tells me. In my time as an aspiring meditator I've learned there's no reason to peek ahead. In fact, there are a lot of reasons not to. Take each breath like the next. Inhale, exhale. Slowly, rhythmically, and quietly. Let the inner chatter and the birdsong intermingle. Let them turn into the soundtrack of one episode. This one. This now you.

That's why sitting quietly matters, to separate your soul from the busyness of days. Perhaps a nap before supper, letting your frozen shoulders relax. Taking time without ear buds or chatter. On the sofa or by a stream. Alone or with others. I don't care if you call it meditating, prayer, or just deep staring. It helps. And it opens you. If you do it more and regularly you'll hear more and better, even if those other channels are muttering along in the background.

Our ancestors knew this kind of listening. Sitting around the fire. Slowing down and calming. Sharing breath and presence. A collective prescience emerging. Then the shamans and teachers and bards would come. Stories and history and legend weaving into a communal blanket. Singers and drummers the heartbeat of the hearth. The hive-mind spread by rituals, before we made Instagram and Twitter.

If you're really trying to soften and heal, to find ways to help the planet and those around you, start by staying present in your life. Confine the binging to TV; make your own world a new episode every day. Every hour. Every minute. Every moment another chance to get it right.

I've studied Tai Chi on and off for decades. It combines healthy movement and spiritual relaxation in the ways that speak to me best, stillness in motion. My current teacher starts class with ten minutes of standing practice. Eyes gently closed, just shifting your weight back and forth, left to right, front and back, until you find the centered place of balance, and become a column of light suspended between earth and sky.

Standing there quietly and gently is a wonderful way to get grounded, to get in touch with your body, and to slow down your mind. It works just like more formal seated meditation and seems to have great physiological benefits to boot.

Try doing this any time of day or night, when you are agitated and need some calm, or when you are feeling soft and grounded and want to see how deep you can go. Just set a timer for ten minutes and let yourself stand suspended in time, on the earth but not so of the world, gently aware of your body but not so tightly tied to it. Let everything relax and settle. You can work your way to longer if you love it, but try this for a week and notice what you feel.

Artisanal You

Decades ago I taught intro statistics for the local community college. In addition to wages, I got to take a free class. I chose hand-building pottery, which means you play like a three-year old with a blob of infinitely malleable clay that you can shape and reshape with no skill beyond your imagination. It is primal and satisfying, and far easier than watercolors, which I abandoned after a term.

It turns out that reshaping ourselves after we commit fully to the process is more successful than our half-hearted attempts. The secret: If you like and trust yourself, you're most of the way there, all the messy details of daily life notwithstanding. You're the clay and the artist, so you can revel in loving your best parts and reshaping the rest. Would that it happened so easily. *Scientific American* blogger Scott Barry Kaufman posted a fabulous summary of the creative process, which directly parallels this work. The stages were: "This is awesome. This is tricky. This is shit. I am shit. This might be okay. This is awesome." I'd be shocked if you haven't been through that cycle several times on this journey. Once you've survived the first few rounds, I hope you'll remember how things shift if you stay on track even a little better than you'd been doing.

Some days you might wake up snarky and feel flat, frustrated, and generally out of sorts. Not a you to build a life upon, because those moods feel like crap; even we want to flee. But we all have them, and sometimes get stuck where they land us. The good news is that we usually unstick ourselves before too very long. Or someone else kicks our butts and gets us moving, whether we're happy about it in the moment or not. I try to remember to say "Thanks" later.

Creating your artisanal self is the ultimate jeans store of life. Sometimes you show off a saggy butt or thunder thighs, or feel everything's tight in all the wrong places. Sometimes you're comfy, other times sexy. When you find the you that you're happy being, it fits just how you want. But you can't know what's right for you unless you've tried on lots of ways to think, believe, and live. That's what all the questions and journaling has been about: to help you decide what the best you wants and feels like. Please, please, don't sell yourself short; don't settle for *I can live with this*. There's a better and happier you still to be created.

How you get to awesome is the land of mystery we've been travelling through. When you wake up happy and curious more often than not you'll notice something has shifted. You're in that other side landscape again, but now it's begun to feel like home. You know with a simple clarity that you're arriving. You feel good, strong, even occasionally fabulous. You don't sweat the small stuff. You know without wondering that your favorite color is purple, that you can stop trying to be friends with the mean girl, and that no matter how well someone prepares tempeh, you simply don't like it no matter how good it is for you. You've earned the right to choose.

I heard a great story about a late-night radio host whom people call for help. She listens to their problems, gives them coaching and support, and then plays a song she chooses for that moment. It's clear she's a people person, making a living doing her favorite things. A great example of why the life coaches always say, "Follow your passion." She was completely her wacky self: owning it, loving it, smiling with the sheer joy of sharing the person she'd invented. Even her war stories were told with a devilish grin, never dwelling on regrets, sorrows, or could-have-beens. You felt happy for her choices and inspired to be bolder making your own.

That's how I want my life to feel, and how I want yours to feel too.

Happiness isn't like the leaden cape you wear for X-rays. It won't shield you from incoming trauma or occasionally feeling like you should've said no to a particularly bad or scary ride. But true happiness means you're willing to trust it. That you don't believe life is a zero-sum game, in which something good in your life, say a joyous new relationship, will be cancelled out by something bad like a car wreck. You can walk around believing it's all going to be okay, maybe not every instant but in the long-run and maybe soon. You're not waiting for some cosmic shoe to drop *Extremely Loud and Incredibly Close,* as Jonathan Safran Foer called 9/11. It's hard to live a full and open life when you're waiting for something to squelch it.

Being happy is partly about feeling safe enough to believe that things in your sphere will lean towards the good. But trusting the universe also means keeping your heart more open than you may be used to. That means risking more vulnerability, less control, and still believing your newfound sense of self will guide you through whatever messy realities you land in. That it will help you through difficulties with greater assurance and less hassle, and steer you to outcomes that support your best and highest good. You may feel things more deeply, perhaps cry more often. But happy people are present, honest, and authentic, as best they can be, in each present moment. Their ability to make good decisions regardless of bad circumstances, and their faith in themselves and the universe, is what guides them. They do not feel alone because they know they belong, that they are on the right path.

A dozen years or so ago, before the farm-to-table movement took over food branding, we were flooded with artisanal everything. The word connoted good bread, craft beer, and heirloom tomatoes: the makings of a fine summer meal. Creating an artisanal you is part of the mission statement of this time around, though you may have long forgotten that your soul wrote one. Most of ours say: If you're doing your karmic homework, regularly swab your lower decks hard (even those murky corners), and are willing to say, *This is who I am and this is what I think, believe, and care about,* you've earned a seat at life's picnic, in all its ant-filled glory. I hope you're closer to that than when we met. Because once you are, you'll start craving that sense of yourself the way you once may have lusted for wine or chocolate. Bonus prize: once the dark and gnarly bits are just old memories, you'll realize you've been liking yourself for a while.

When you pack your picnic basket, don't choose all sweets. You may not like sour or bitter, but in the right proportions they add dimension. Yes, too, to savory and spice and to the elusive umami. They create a robust palette for our senses, and add savoring to our skill set. Create a menu from a planet of possibilities, not just the happy meal you ate when you were five. We need the whole range to become our whole selves.

I hope your life is juicy with whatever flavors you have a hankering for. Enjoy these moments, each and every one, when they show up, whether it's a day or even a minute, alone or with family and friends. Put that feeling of trust into the marrow of you so you can find it whenever you need to.

I don't want to sound selfish. We're here to be nurturing, generous, and kind, as well as individually happy. It truly matters how we treat others, or the world becomes angry and divided, which hurts us all. If you doubt me, look at fanatics of every stripe and everyone they impact. But you have to take good care of yourself to make a better world. Like the old slogan "Think Global, Act Local," make your personal microcosm good; you'll spread goodness instead of fear. The changes start inside you, and work their way out as far as you're willing to reach.

One day I realized I was ten pounds heavier than I'd sworn ever again to weigh. But I was happy—extra pounds be damned. I could say that because I liked the Helen I had become. I was living off the bounty of good decisions. I could imagine my world continuing to improve, and I trusted that weight loss would be part of the process, not a necessary precondition. For too long I had measured happiness by externals, like "after my doctoral exams," or "after I'm in a good relationship," or "after I lose weight." Getting happier took lots of trial and error, because life changes don't come with nice clean edges. For most of us, real change takes many tries, but, amazingly, they finally feel embedded. I had transformed my insides. Now I could successfully reinvent my outsides.

They say we use only about ten percent of our brain. I hope that's not true about our authentic selves, that we only let ten percent of who we are show. It would be such a waste. The world would be so much duller and less interesting.

When I was young and butchering piano lessons, the teacher wanted me to learn one little music-box piece, so I could have mastery over something. It wasn't completely hopeless but pretty darn close; I felt tone deaf and clumsy. Years later I found my instrument, which feels natural and graceful and which I play with joy instead of angst and struggle. I hope you've found your favorite ways to be, whether that's gardening or teaching, kayaking or governing. I hope you're on a road that matters to you, and that you feel like you're getting somewhere.

For a long time I had an ongoing metaphor of becoming Helen 3.0. It was a living story. I knew I was emerging into a different phase of life. I'd made intentional and sometimes difficult choices to earn that, so I thought consciously about who and how Helen 3.0 would be. And slowly I morphed into her. Not abruptly, but consistently, and reasonably fast compared to the painful slowness of earlier transitions and the long times of feeling stuck.

It's a shame it takes us so long to figure out who we are. Maybe not in the multi-incarnational notion of time, but in our human ways of measuring. Life helps us strip away all the extra coatings, the *klipot* I spoke about earlier. On the healing road we mend our tender places so they no longer hurt so badly. Now when I think about those littlest dolls,

I realize they're okay, not as tender or easily bruised. Once they grokked that they were loved and welcomed they could grow into their vibrant, beautiful selves. And that happened because I was ready, and because I said *Yes* as often as I needed to, and *No* when it was the right answer.

One night I journalled, "I can be trusted." It wasn't about navigating the world, being a good employee or partner, or making good decisions at the store. It was the much bigger realization that I'd been a good guide for myself. That I'd led me to becoming Helen 3.0 and that I liked being her. Helen 3.0 is wise and funny and smart. She knows what she likes (and what she doesn't) without much fussing. She's more open, listens better, and embraces what she loves without ambivalence. I'm not beyond struggles, but I'm ready to respond in new ways to their challenges: by doing this work, and living by what I sincerely believe is a valuable set of transformational tools. The questions still bubble up. But I'm able to answer more clearly, more simply, with a deeper understanding of where the questions come from and where the answers lead. After my perspective shifted I saw an indistinct figure on the horizon. She moved with vision and purpose. And I realized that beyond now was Helen 4.0. I'm looking forward to creating and getting to know her too.

I hope you're finding enough perspective, even vista, that you can appreciate the whole of life's journey and see where you fit in. That you see the road as more than one rocky patch at a time. That you enjoy triumphant progress often enough to get you through the next tough phase. That you do not feel alone: that you have found love, and friendship, and a sense of kinship with your tribe, however you define that. I hope you can imagine your next evolution. Not by forcing your world to meet some preconceived image, but by dancing with it, seeing the ley lines and the flow of your life as the map you were making way back when.

There's room in this world for any you that you want to become: CEO or cowgirl. Mother, lover, healer, artist, whatever you can imagine. You create this life by your intention and by living with all the authenticity that you're willing to put into the world.

Our dreams of who we can become are what make us rise each morning and greet the sun with curiosity and wonder. Sure on a bad or gnarly day, you wonder why you even peeked through the blinds. But on one of those days when you glimpse something that shines, when you feel it connect in some wondrous way with the holy spark inside of you, there's an elevation. With that we come away a little bit sweeter, kinder, and happier. We smile more at one another and ourselves. We are generous with exactly the gentleness with which we wish to be greeted.

One night I imagined my next incarnation, and thought about what I'd bring along if I could, what I'd change, what I hoped was finally resolved, and what I'd leave to chance.

Try this some evening when you're feeling fine, after a particularly good but gentle day. Ruminate, perhaps with a nightcap or some candles. Feel it, write it down, and let in. Be in the life you want to live. Grok it in a truly visceral way.

Then ask how much of that you could create while you're here with us now.

You will find great delight in becoming that you sooner than you might even expect. And I suspect the rest of us will like knowing her too.

YOU, ME, US

Stories are webs, interconnected strand to strand, and you follow each story to the center, because the center is the end. Each person is a strand of the story.
—NEIL GAIMAN

Pull a thread here and you'll find it's attached to the rest of the world.
—NADEEM ASLAM

Loves Me, Loves Me Not

Love is the most important, fragile, and mysterious of human emotions. I can't imagine a world without it. I want a world where love rules.

We count on those we love to hug us when we hurt, to listen and to tell us hard truths, and to warn us before we do something that will hurt even more. There are so many kinds of loving relationships. Friends you've known forever and friends who feel that way. New friends who surprise and delight you. The ones where you can be 100% yourself, without worrying about bad patterns, boundaries, or taboos. Lovers and partners and spouses and sometimes even exes. Inter-generational buddies. Parent/child/nana, teacher/student, penpal, and a zillion more. The *Pick up. I need you now!* bestie you can't imagine life without. And yes, some folks may be in several of these roles.

Meeting those special people is among life's biggest gifts. From the very beginning you know them in a deep, swift, and simple way. It's energetic, electric, and satisfying, with a resonance that's welcoming, exciting, and expansive. You're smiling, anticipating a world you don't yet know but that your heart tells you will be good.

It may take a while to sort out the who-we-are-this-time pieces, but your souls have agreed to meet and do some work together. "Work" may involve laughter, kissing, talking, and occasionally getting smashed and staying up all night solving the world's ills and your own. These friendships take you places you might not dare to go alone, but because you're with your buddy you'll be brave. Your time together will almost certainly involve vulnerability, tears, and helping one another unload old stories that no longer serve you, as well as facing and solving the various crises and hassles of now. If you're lucky that is.

The people to whom you can entrust your heart are the most important ones in your life. If not, they should be. Sometimes the friendship is delicious and sweet and makes you feel invincible, at least for a while. You might want it to last forever. For the rare and blessed it actually does. You may know them or have heard their stories: *We met and I knew right away. I've loved her every day since.* Who doesn't long for that kind of love?

Sometimes we're here to share tougher lessons. They rarely come with even a hint of fun, unless you count scary detours and crash-and-burn sideshows. We meet for a growth spurt; we wrestle with our tangled karma; and then we part, occasionally on good terms but more often not. Sometimes those very folks or their doppelgängers show up again later, and we have to decide if we need another dose of that same lesson. And sometimes we get spooked. We see their echoes in different people, and have to work harder to see new folks for who they really are. It's hard not to carry old cautions when your heart has been bruised. Even if some moments are rocky, what matters most is that you soften and open, and that you learn from your pain. That's how we heal.

I couldn't be as good a me if I didn't have you to push against, listen to, think about, and help. If I didn't have caring folk to do the same for me, my life would be far poorer. Your needs and challenges mirror mine. If we're lucky our crises won't coincide, so we can support one another, cheering in the good times and holding each other in the bad ones. We're playing together in the karmic kitchen: cooking up our futures, testing life's recipes, seeing what we like and don't, and trusting our buddies to remember, remind us, and kick us in the butt when we need it most. One of my best friends and I call each other "essence friends." She gave me among the best gifts I've ever received over our shared Taurus birthday dessert: she made the wish over her very own birthday candle about the success of this book. In *Grey's Anatomy* terms, when you and a friend look at one another and say, "You're my person," it's a commitment as deep as any "I do."

With perspective and the blessing of time, I can even value those who made my journey harder or more annoying, because they carried lessons I needed to work through. For most of us, those less joyous relationships include exes, bosses, relatives, and even some friends. For mine, I think I've settled my karmic debts; if not I'll risk the IOU.

Mostly it feels good to like folks and be liked back. To be seen and valued and to offer that in return. Friendship is a great place to set the bar, and transcends the vicissitudes of romantic relationships. But we're all hungry for love, and in seeking it we've all made mistakes we wish we could erase. They're counterbalanced by the folks we've found that we can trust with our hearts, our sanity, and even our lives. I've never been a soldier, but I respect band-of-brothers loyalty, mirrored by the love of parents for their children. In her brilliant novel *Circe*, Madeline Miller describes the perspective of a mother looking at her newborn, "I would look at him and feel a love so sharp it seemed my flesh lay open. I made a list of all the things I would do for him. Scald off my skin. Tear out my eyes. Walk my feet to bones, if only he would be happy and well." I share that kind of bond with a special few. I cannot imagine life without them.

There are many kinds of love. But the romantic dyad is the one most adults focus on. That may be the most difficult, persistent, and optimistic endeavor that we engage in as humans. Rom-coms, sitcoms, dramas, and tragedies are filled with the angst and craziness of how we search for love, and all the ways it can go wrong, modeled in every age, gender, and circumstance you can imagine. We watch and cheer, groan, commiserate, and weep while we drink in those stories. They help us see that no one gets it right the first time, or even the third, and that love's only pretty in central casting.

Falling in love was easy when we were teenagers because hormones ran the show. As we age, our tastes become more refined; our opinions on politics, class, religion, and more help to quickly narrow the field. These times offer an explosion of dating sites, with questionnaires about everything from food prefs to kinks. We can cruise online profiles the way librarians browse books. There are I-have-a-friend-I-think-you'd-like blind dates and random meetings in the market, a class, a gathering, or a ball game. But no matter how hard folks try to find love, the best connections often happen when you stop looking. Some combination of dumb luck, karmic timing, and being ready for whatever lessons that new relationship will bring.

No matter how you meet, little in life rivals the messy joys of falling in love. Most of us care about little except when we'll next be together. Infinite touching and all the spontaneous treats, cutesy emoticons, little gifts, and sweet nothings. Being hungry for your new honey 24/7, and wishing the world would just be quiet and let you two alone to glow. There's a desire for connection that happens when we're learning another person that seems almost frantic. A need to fuse energy, smell, and skin. Making love, a delicious and luxuriant gateway. Note: I'll never bet against sensuality as a teacher, with chords as resonant and powerful as prayer. Falling in love is a magical land where rules don't apply. At least in the beginning.

New love alters time. For most of us the first month is a tsunami of exploring and delight, every cell in our body straining for connection. Random "sick days" to snuggle or go off on an adventure. Laughter and stories, the good ones to start with, with the occasional mild confession tossed in as a litmus test. Midnight pizza and ice cream. Learning who makes better coffee or breakfast. Walking around with big chunks in the dreamland of desire. There are no boundaries; you haven't even started thinking about them. There's desire, hope, and a deep yearning. As a new love once said, "I want you to reach into my heart in a certain way." I hope you've had those times and remember them sweetly.

If only it lasted forever. If we didn't have to put on our grown-up clothes, go do things like earn a living, pay bills, or talk to people about things other than our new true love. Yes, that's my inner romantic speaking. What makes it special is exactly that it doesn't last.

In the times that follow we start to learn one another. We share our stories: who our people are, what makes us tick, what we adore and detest, and what we're dreaming of. Also (spoken or not), what we hope this relationship might become. As we listen to what comes towards us, we start seeing our new love's best and worst qualities. We discern depth and judgment. We see this person is good and trustworthy, someone with whom we might build a life. That s/he is kind, caring, gentle, generous, smart, funny, and reliable. Or not. We may see a selfish or judgmental side, perhaps narcissism or even cruelty.

We also begin to notice what may drive us nuts later. We remember that an old adage, "What you love most in the beginning is what you'll hate most at the end" is often true. I'm not just talking about small annoyances like knuckle cracking or soup slurping, but the bigger issues. Like when you ask "How are you with money?" and your new honey almost crashes the car. A partner who hates your cooking or a lover who doesn't get your sexual cues. For some folks it's true love until they die and the minor things be damned. But for most of us, relationships from dating through marriage, divorce, and all the way back to dating again, are experiments at balancing what we want, what we need, what we can live with, and what's less than we deserve or should tolerate.

Helen's first two rules of dating, painfully earned: *I only want to be with someone who wants to be with me. Choose wisely.*

It's important to create equity early on. Sure, some folks are better at certain things, from cleaning to vacation planning, but roles that become entrenched from the outset will almost inevitably cause friction over time. So-and-so always drives or chooses the movie, restaurant, or which friends to visit. We're always at my place or we never are. She forgot her wallet again. Each of us gets to, and has to, decide what the deal-breakers are, what we're willing to compromise on, and what is a necessary ingredient for emotional health.

Control is a big issue, which can easily turn into power struggles or game playing when things go south. You can learn a lot about your newly beloved before things settle into patterns. And you should. If I ran the world, partners would take turns surprising one another on alternate dates, limited only by their imagination and basic constraints of reality. They would learn each other through that kind of sharing. Dating also helps us learn how to make room for another person in our world. Among life's ironies is how often you hear someone say, "Just when I'd stopped looking...." or "My life is too busy for a relationship," and poof, you've tempted the gods once too often, and they send you the person bearing kisses, along with whatever you most need to learn next.

Eventually things settle down and you see the whole picture of whom you've chosen, in all their flaws and glory. Not to make you self-conscious, but they're looking at you the same way. And there's no use being on company behavior. Because if you can't be completely comfortable being yourself, why bother being together? There's a fabulous meme that goes roughly, "If you lost it by being honest, you never really had it." Voices may get brisker, even testy, for toilet seats left up or a favorite shirt shrunk in the wash. I'm more tidy than antiseptic, and woe to anyone who'd need me very long as a nurse. Those might be deal-killers for some folks. For me, the bigger must-haves revolve around communication, integrity, and intimacy. I'm willing to negotiate the small things, but only with the right person, one that I trust with my heart and soul. We can sort out the little annoyances while we talk.

We've all got our preferences and desires. Dating profiles are filled with them. But no algorithm can substitute for honesty and trust. My third and final rule of dating: *I only want to be with someone who adores my best qualities, and tolerates my worst ones with patience and humor.*

I love being around happy couples that are clearly partnered for life. They know how to disagree, even have the occasional raucous fight. But they don't damage one another in the process. They argue, apologize, clear the air, and forgive. Unless you're among those fortunate ones, love almost always causes pain along with growth.

Virtually every relationship develops quiet pockets. That's how we don't kill each other, as you might wish to do with annoying strangers, like the person at your gym who grunts too loudly and often. But with folks you really care about, it's easy to develop bad patterns: going light when you should press about something that just doesn't sit right. It's emotionally safer, and avoids arguments, but it has big downsides in the long run. I had a bestie of years drift away because we never learned how to argue and get back on track, and I lost another because words said in anger were too hard to un-hear. With folks we trust we can go to the mat, say the hard truths, and come back to caring and having fun. It keeps the relationship open and growing. Otherwise, what looks like parallel paths can too easily diverge, and the space between fill with irreconcilable gaps. Honest communication depends upon mutual respect, upon listening, and ultimately on being willing to say "I'm wrong" and "I'm sorry." I think forgiveness, real and sincere, is built into the foundation of every happy couple. Both of you need to practice all of these or the relationship can easily become emotionally unhealthy. It sounds like work, and it can be. But if you make love and laugh often, talk like good friends, and give each other space to be individuals as well as part of a dyad, there is lots of room for magic.

In a relationship that's not on track, something eventually wakes us up. Something important inside us feels lost or dimmer. It's like phantom limb syndrome: what's missing hurts and we want it back. First we look for what's wrong, the way we'd search for our missing phone, taking a careful inventory of everywhere we've been. Our urgency or reticence is determined by which emotional toes got stepped on, and how often and hard. Slowly we realize that we feel less like us, that we're not as happy as we were. That's not compared to the heady zap of falling in love, but rather to who you were before the relationship and to the self you were on track to becoming. It's akin to what astronauts must feel as they reenter gravity: suddenly everything is heavier and you can no longer fly free on a whim. Unless you've really blown it—by picking a thief or an ax murderer—this usually happens far more gradually. But there are other bad choices, from what one friend calls "an energy vampire" to what I've experienced as an emotional black hole.

Like the frog in the cooking pot that doesn't jump out as the water very slowly heats, you may stay far too long in a situation that is not good for you. Many of us have, and have been known to do it again. In my life, what I've regretted most was not speaking up when I knew things weren't right or good for me. I wish I'd had the courage to change or end those relationships so much sooner.

Without mutual trust and kindness, relationships falter and eventually crash. Or else folks stay in ones that have become an empty husk. They're marking time, wondering what went wrong, why they've stayed, and if it's too late to start over. Too often, fear of the unknown trumps a willingness to speak up and say, "I think we need to work on this. Do you care enough to try?" I wish I had. Instead I mostly muddled through, thinking I knew what I was doing.

I had a bad "picker" when I was younger, so repeated some mistakes. But the lessons I did learn got hammered in hard and still guide me. The ones I had to repeat are integrated too, with a twinge of annoyance at my slow learning curve. I want those years back. Sigh. I suspect your emotional history has similar low and high points. Very few of us get off easy in affairs of the heart. The best we can hope for is to learn, and keep our hearts open instead of armored.

Recently I was talking with a close friend about love. She was in a new relationship but something felt not right. We went through all the variations of *Am I jumping too soon? What if I stay too long? Is this as good as it gets? What's wrong with me?* and *What if I end up alone?* My only solace to her: we don't get it all in one person. We're hardwired to want it that way, but it's rare and it probably should be. The problem is that when we don't feel well-met in the places that matter to us most, we get confused, angry, guilty, and surprisingly embarrassed. Like a recipe gone wrong, sometimes we need to start over instead of adding a little more of this and that, trying to fix it like a dish that's too salty or sour. That may not mean jumping ship, though the temptation to cut off things cleanly is always there. But a necessary start is clear and honest communication. That's the baseline to build upon. If it works, hooray. If not, perhaps you can say goodbye without blame or recrimination.

Almost everyone in a long-term relationship sacrifices something. Sometimes it is simple, like not cooking with cilantro. But sometimes it's a tradeoff that others might consider too great a sacrifice. One may want children and the other not. Some folks give up sex for a settled partnership. Others give up security to feel young and hot again. Sex and money are two big things folks struggle about and sometimes give up, but the subtler ones can be just as important and equally destructive: not feeling heard or loved, being taken for granted, not sharing language or values about spirituality, politics, and social issues. People give up different things not to be alone. And for some folks being single is the simplest and happiest choice of all.

The Hebrew word for heart is *lev*, so close to *love*. The end of a great love, whether it's your idea, mutual, or thrust upon you, hurts your heart in a literal ache. Heartbreak can hurt worse than a migraine, though I hope both are few for you. No matter how well your friends take care of you, or say you're better off without him or her, you will need to endure this time. It's rarely pleasant, even if you're happy that the relationship has ended.

Healing can be painfully slow but trying to fast forward just kicks the problem into your future. You're wise not to be tempted by a rebound quickie, unless a hot landing zone is all you want. But eventually, slowly as it may have seemed, it will feel like your healing is happening on scar tissue and not in a void. There's a foundation to bond to. You start to hurt less and eventually you don't. You'll notice you can't re-member when you stopped crying, and that you're laughing more. You may still have maudlin moments, but if you can avoid drinking and dialing (like in the movie *Sideways*), you'll eventually unplug from the past, and find the optimism to try love again.

Sometimes our lives just move apart. Friend or lover, it's just not as personal as it used to be. No big fight or event. Just a slow, quiet dimming of the connection that you handle more easily than you ever thought possible. As we become more our evolving selves, our lives become bright with new people. They show us what we most need now. The ones we knew way back when will always hold a piece of us, but it's like an artifact from a world that is no more. We can still follow and know about one another via social media, but it's not the same deep connecting as it was. We have memories, good and bad, and that's mostly enough. If it's not, pay attention and dig deeper into why you're hanging on and what you still want and need from this person. Then lean in or let go as your heart will prompt you.

We need friends who share our soul language. Because ultimately love is about connection, whether it is romantic or platonic. When we share it, there's no better feeling in the world. It doesn't matter if that person will live with us and clean up the puke, as long as they see us, hear us, understand us, and love us. That kind of love lights up the world. I hope you have known it and that it has nourished and sustained you. I hope it helped you to grow and become happier. I wish you an abundance of feeling seen, heard, loved, and appreciated for your thoroughly glorious self.

I hope those you love can hear even when you're silent, and that you can feel them whenever they send you loving thoughts, no matter how far away they are. Because that is how we will heal this planet. By loving one another so fiercely and so well that we overcome the negativity that threatens to diminish us as a people, a species, and perhaps a planet.

Who are your people?

Who do you love, trust, and listen to, whether they're telling you something you want to hear or very much don't?

With whom do you feel completely safe when you are emotionally naked, soul-to-soul?

Who knows all your old secrets? With whom can you share every new embarrassment and folly with laughter and rueful knowing instead of hiding it in shame?

Do you say "I love you" to them regularly, with sincerity and hugs? If not, say it more often with words and hugs.

WHEN THE BOUGH BREAKS

We all face death, though usually we look away. Dying means loss. Whether it's someone we know and care about, or after a Sandy Hook and the too many and too frequent similar tragedies, we feel helpless in our grief. Last autumn I had two friends with almost identical symptoms. One skates away benign and we bury the other four months later. Why?

In his brilliant Holocaust novel, *The Seventh Well*, Fred Wander describes death in a Nazi work camp. Prisoners are staked within running distance of the woods and possible freedom. They are not tethered, fed, or given water, but are made to stand until they collapse and die, or choose to run and be shot. Each lives with imminent death for days. The ultimate existential choice: each second they choose the pain of living instead of bolting for a quick end. Sadly, it's not unique. Unless the pain is unbearable, and sometimes even then, we cling fiercely to life. After the doctor told my mother he could not save her and disconnected her oxygen, she lived another forty-two hours. She hadn't made it twelve hours off the vent in the three weeks before. Biology or soul, most of us choose life.

Some do not. I've known people who chose, or seriously contemplated, an early death when facing a diagnosis that portended losing what made them feel like themselves. Others living lives that seemed worse than whatever lies beyond have left us early, because going on seemed more than they could bear. And others found acceptance in surrendering to the inevitable that we all face, preferring the dignity of choice about when and how they would transition. What felt right to them might make no sense to others, but was their choice. I mourn not just their pain and despair, but the loss and sorrow experienced by those who loved them.

A friend's mother died recently. Amid the condolences and dinner invites, what I most wanted to say was, "Take good notes," because when my own mother died it was such a blur of feelings and doings. Admittedly, "Take good notes" is a baseline as advice to self and others goes, in good times and in bad. As is "Pay better attention," and (in my mother's voice), "Stand up straight." I still blush remembering her never-subtle public prompts, replete with drill sergeant shoulders and a look that burned a path through crowds. But her death was a cascade of feelings that dwarf deconstruction.

I was curious if my friend would have great insights into mortality. She's older than I was when my mom died, and we're both ages that you see in the obits and no longer think, *Oh so young.* More like, *I hope she had a good life.* We're at a time when you fear there's much less life left than you once hoped, and can imagine choosing less time over other more difficult options. Aging brings worse fears too, and a gentle passing sounds like a lovely ride out.

Most of us spend little time thinking about death. Except perhaps after a close call, or if we are docs, lawyers, or recently diagnosed. But we regular folk go through our days assuming life will be as it is: long, fruitful, and happy. We probably spend more time paying bills each month than thinking about mortality. It's more than dodging pain, suffering, or losing those we love. We don't like things so out of our control, or the idea of not being here ourselves.

I've been accused of liking life comfortable. So it was a shock, and a curious mix of "Winter is coming..." and an unexpected spiritual graduation gift, that just when I was feeling happiest, most creative, and quite proud of myself for various chunks of personal progress that the doors of change swung wide open. That month we had a horrible ice storm. Freezing rain coated every bud, twig, and branch. Trees bowed low to the ground, and two of my oldest and tallest were uprooted and fallen. My garden was a landscape forever transformed, cleft open, and all too silent and still. I was lucky—no smashed roof or car, no dangling power line. Just an expensive mess, a denuded yard, and a week without Wi-Fi.

The storm hit as a wonderful woman I knew was dying, a brilliant, stubborn, witty, old Jewess, who had battled social injustice and cancer with the same fierce necessity. She had a stroke and slipped away within hours. An "easy death." So did my tall pine. Falling slowly, cushioned by a faithful crab apple; interwoven wisteria vines guiding her tip to rest gently on the house. I'd planted that tree three decades before, and was bereft by the sudden loss. So big; so long with me; so quick to transform.

When someone close to us dies we feel the same. We're in a different world than the one we shared with the departed. In one world they're sharing a meal and a laugh. In another they are memory. They answer our questions and stories with cryptic silence, or too brief and rare a glimpse in a dream. They are gone. We move forward and they do not. We're in the world; they're off duty. Off to their next assignment, whatever it is, maybe with a little R&R in between. I'm not sure how it works, and I'm willing to learn when it's my time.

I was in my late twenties before anyone close to me died—a side effect of excellent genetics. The loss was my cat, most likely to a coyote. But we lived together for years in a Los Angeles canyon, and it was my first direct encounter with mortality. I went to a Chinese herbalist. He spoke little English, so I said simply, "My best friend died." He gave me two large, paper-wrapped packets: herbs, twigs, seeds, shells, dust, and moss, that I was to boil down to a cup of sludge, two days in a row. Plus, a laughably few raisins to clear the taste. On the afternoon of the second day, I literally collapsed into tears. A torrential weeping of decades, all my early unshed tears and so many unshed since. Not for another decade would I have that profound a release.

You're never ready to lose a parent. Even with lots of notice or if you've been through it before. It hurts and it sucks and there's no court of appeal. After my mother's funeral I went to services to say *kaddish* (the Jewish prayer for the dead). The woman sitting behind me sang off-key exactly like my mother, which felt like a visitation from The Great Beyond. A few years later, at a big fork in my road, I had another visitation from my mother. As I sat in my car contemplating a huge life change, I felt the hairs on the back of my neck stand up, and half-suspected that I might see her if I turned to look at the back seat. After almost twenty years, whenever I discover an author she'd like or make a fabulous pot of soup, I still feel the urge to call her. If I had one more day with her, I'd spend it in the kitchen, asking so many questions and watching all those lost secrets. She taught me many things, most good and comforting, though some hobbled me in ways it took years to undo.

My mother took good care of my dad, at clear costs to herself. He could tell a good joke, usually as a wry observer. He loved to chat with folks most people ignore, like waiters and the staff in his assisted living center, often in French or Spanish. But he was usually laconic on the phone. After my mother's death I became his designated listener. He loved to answer saying, "Anything else?" Few believed me when I said we had long conversations about Wimbledon and politics. I remember sitting together, he newly transplanted from their home after her death, cheering as Gore won Florida. (Don't get me started...)

Every transition includes loss of the known, the familiar, and the illusion of control. You can shake your fist but still death comes. You can grovel, beg, and plead, but your loved one will still die. As unfair or untimely or simply unwanted as that may be, it is also inevitable. We can rant and hate it all we like.

In this universe, the us we are used to being is 100% mortal. The physical envelope wears out, but the soul not so much, which is why I keep saying snuggle up and make friends with your immortal parts. Learn to find your truest self, even and perhaps especially in hard or confusing times. Because that's when you'll need her most. Find your inner North Star so you have something to navigate by.

When the human you have been, and the you that you feel you are slides off, your soul goes on to new adventures, released and rejuvenated (pun intended), you'll get another of those glimpses, a remembering of your true self, until you start that story anew, and get tangled in its humanness.

My simple rant on death: It sucks. It is nasty and implacable and impossible to satisfy. It takes the ones we love and gives us only memory in return. That seems such a feeble bargain. We know we've been had and there's no one to complain to.

Death's partner time does much of what comes next. The slow dulling, the silent erasure of memory, fewer glimpses even further apart. Unless, like a faithful widower, we tend the memory, bringing flowers and parking by the grave for a chat. Eventually that might bring comfort, but it takes a while, and there's lots of sadness and missing between one to the other.

What I most want to do to death is what June Squibb does to an ex's grave in *Nebraska*, lifting her skirt and shouting defiance. She's alive and laughing; he missed all the fun. Instead we grovel and beg: *Another year. A few more months.* We bargain even when we have nothing to ante. Most of us don't know how to let go gracefully. For all the messiness, we want as much as we can get of this life and want it for all those we care about.

I've wept over pets as much as people, for their unconditional love, and judgment only when we're slow with treats or opening a door. Among life's wisest teachings came from my vet: "They'll tell you when it's time." Years later, when my old boy was so thin and ready for release, she said, "He's like a prisoner scratching at the lock and you have the key."

We don't usually get to turn that key for ourselves or those we care about. That decision is taken away by illness or age or distracted drivers, to name but a few. It can come out of nowhere. It's a beautiful sunny day, you're watching spring bloom all around you; then a friend calls to say, "The biopsy's back," and bursts into tears. Suddenly your universe slips a cog or three in a terrible direction, and the life you knew is spinning away faster than you could ever call it back. Your heart just got shattered and stomped on hard.

Most of us don't do the death dance well. Death ignores our wailing and shaking of fists. We hate every minute it's happening and hate the silence it leaves behind. It hurts like hell to let go. To know you can never again just pick up the phone and dial. No texting or stories or hot wonderful sex. No laughter by the fire and rituals of companionship. Not one more hug. Maybe they can see us, but most of us don't know how to see back through the veil. I rely on the quaint simplicity of Billy Collins's poem *The Dead,* which tells us they still care, even if we cannot see them.

But in real time it is painful and raw. Not just after they're gone, but from the moment the dreaded words are spoken and our world turns sideways. The horrid clinical phrases that measure our days mask the simplest truth: a countdown clock is ticking for us all, and there's only one door. This happened to one of my dearest as I wrote this book. My stomach was a knot for weeks before I could let myself feel the truth of it. To accept I'd likely be here and she would not. I struggled with this quote from Sengai, a Zen artist and poet: "It is no patience which you can bear patiently. Patience is to bear what is unbearable."

Some day, people will mourn you as you have mourned. They'll be in their version of this story and there'll be a hole where once you were. Perhaps a sore place they'll bump into.

A sound, image, or place that evokes you as they feel sorrow and longing in that place named you in their heart. In Judaism when someone dies, we say, "May his/her memory be for a blessing." Like the movie *CoCo* made so beautifully vivid, no one is completely dead until all memories of them are gone.

In this inexorable accounting, there is one sure truth. Keep sharing love and comfort. Keep your heart open as best you can for as long as you're here. Keep folks around that you love and that love you back: the deep heart-to-hearts and the ones who call just to say hi, to let you know they're okay. One of my besties is such. I think that in another time I lost her in the trains as we headed for the death camps. Now she calls just to tug on her end of the string. She'll start a conversation with "I have nothing to say," and we laugh and start to chat. We're different in so many ways, but sisters like the tall pine and the crabapple, sharing our messy joys and silly stories, and are there for each other in a heartbeat the minute either has a need.

Keep those folks around you and hold them close. Tell them you love them more often than you might. Because one day no phone will work. And you'll have to find them all over again the next time around.

For me the ultimate death question is not, When will I go?, but How do I want to live while I'm here?

We're all a nanosecond from the brink. Accident, aging, choice, or disease, we will be gone too soon. So we need to know in our heart of hearts and gut of guts what is worthy of our attention and love.

Do you?

HOME BASE

Iappreciate home with or without other folks around. Company's fun but so is peace and quiet. A friend and I were discussing this recently. She told me about selling her vintage camper, remodeled with splashy good taste. She took the first okay offer, "Because I got tired of having to be nice when people knocked at the door."

I'm not suggesting the world's not filled with fascinating folk. I'm always eager to meet them. I've been delighted to the core by newer friends who've shown up later in life, surprising me with how valuable a place they've claimed in my world and my heart. Later friendships have a depth that shows up more gently, without the fanfare of youth. Lots can be learned kicking back in adjoining chaises, watching cloud pictures in tandem or sitting by a winter fire with a mug of cocoa or tea, as much sitting as talking, letting your rhythms melt together as you knit your bonds.

If you're more of a recluse, you get to winnow the company. Trim the guest list of those you hang with and those you listen to. Choose only to be with the ones you truly value. One of my favorite quotes is from actress Jeanne Moreau, interviewed on *Fresh Air*: "I treasure my solitude because I have the freedom to decide with whom to share it."

One year at the holidays I got into a long discussion with a survivor of childhood sexual abuse. We talked about all the reasons people didn't feel safe in the world, at home, even in their own skin. About the same time I heard a radio story about a security expert; he distinguished between being safe and feeling safe. He pointed out that while we might in fact be safe, if we don't feel safe, we're not.

Part of the journey to self-knowing may mean going exactly where you don't feel safe, even where you may feel afraid. For some folks that might mean skydiving or saying yes to some challenge you fear you're not ready to tackle. For those who've experienced serious traumas, it can mean braving memories and flashbacks as you try to unpack how they have hurt you. You need to believe you can go there emotionally and come home safe and healed. For serious traumas like sexual abuse, the healing may require trained help; it certainly requires the love and ears of trusted friends or folks who've had similar histories. If you make this part of the journey, the you who you become will be stronger than the earlier you, who is herself braver than the you who was afraid to look in that direction, let alone to take the first step. Never discount how serious an undertaking it can be or how necessary a part of your healing doing this work can be, especially if you do not feel safe.

It is only by confronting fear that we shed the layers of armoring and self-protection in which we cocoon ourselves. The layers we are peeling off have served us well and long for a reason. In the past we needed them. Now we are developing a different form of safety, one that derives from our inner strength, not outer barriers, be they emotional or physical.

At the edge of autumn, long sleeves feel natural in the breeze. Not in the sun of course, when one can feel prematurely overdressed. But those rare hot moments are a deep inhalation, taking in what's left of what went by so fast—too fast for those in northern climes, though perhaps those in warmer regions long for cooling rains. After we move inside, we see nature through windows. We brave whatever elements prevail when we're in the world, which feels less welcoming, more of a challenge. In winter we look at nature more than we're in it.

A favorite photograph of my father and his twin brother, aged mid-60s, shows them taking a siesta together in the yard on a chilly November afternoon: both in woolen overcoats, hats, scarves, and two blankets each, tucked toes to chin. They'd been refugees and immigrants, but they always had each other and a twin-like security most of us lack.

I recall sitting with my dad when my mother was dying, talking quietly in the long hours of waiting. I asked him, "When you think about your life, what do you see?" His answer became my baseline for a peaceful life, whatever the struggles of the moment: "I never went hungry. I always slept in a bed. I never had to hold a gun." There's a place to set the bar. If we all had even that.

My politics are lefty liberal. So I tend to blame greed and inequity for many social ills. But imagine if everyone—not just folks you know and folks they know, even going a dozen rings out—had a safe place to sleep, wasn't hungry, had good work, was a good citizen, and had leisure time to do whatever they wanted? Can you imagine what the planet could become?

I heard recently about detection of an interstellar sound wave, possibly from "a higher order intelligence." The definition had something to do with harnessing the power of a distant sun for space travel. Not a guarantee of future visitors, but enough of a sparkle to be worth thinking about. In a *Star Trek* episode, we'd be the planet they landed on, not the *Enterprise* crew. Assume folks (or very not-folks-looking beings, as in the movie *Arrival*) with brain power a hundred or thousand times greater than ours. To them we'd look like tribes of squabbling children, overdue for the time-out corner or possibly worse.

But what if all the things that keep us separated, by religions, countries, and socio-economics, were gone? What if we all started with enough? What might we become and learn?

The other day I had a new sofa delivered. The driver, Luis, asked me about a framed picture of Anne Frank I keep on a wall. I told him her story, all new to him. He told me how his parents came to America, and that he would tell his daughter about Anne Frank, because she could read the famous diary as a break from her dental studies. I reflected what a wonderful American moment it was: two children of immigrants sharing their origin stories.

I think Buddhists get lots of stuff right, and a key thought is this: dualism is bad for the soul. In the worlds of us vs. them, blue states and red, bickering races, nations, and religions, the world gets harsh much too quickly and stays there much too angrily. What if we were all part of us? And how the @#$%& do we get there?

In this journey you have so many choices. Like the eternal battle between your *yetzer hatov* and *yetzer hara*, your better and worse aspects, there are lots of pushes and pulls. Your inner light and your unconsciousness run in shifts, deciding where to go based on how safe or needy you feel in any given situation. Each thinks the direction they've chosen is right and that any other option is wrong. When you want the world just for you and the ones you pick, you're starting down a regressive road, not moving forward. We talk about God as oneness, sufficiency, safety, and love. Rabbi David Cooper wisely calls God "a verb." We need to make more doorways to peace; my vote is through awe and gratitude. Jews debate whether "awe" connotes fear, or whether it's the vulnerability and openness that comes from recognizing energies far greater than our own. I'm rooting for wonder. Haven't we all had enough fear? Dues paid. Move on. Enough with the fighting and otherness. Enough with needing to feel bigger because you've made someone else feel small.

What if we could transcend winners and losers? What if we didn't look at life like a zero-sum game where you feared my happiness comes at a cost to you? It doesn't and it never did. I wish you much more happiness and much less fear and anger. But how do we achieve and share this consciousness without needing a common enemy?

I think it starts with two old men lying out in the cold, unafraid of the elements and secure in their lives, trusting in the simplest way. No mantra or mudra or special prayer. Just taking a nap in the fading autumn sun and assuming they'll wake up safe.

Next time you're tempted to speak in frustration or anger, hit the pause button. Instead of fighting, take a nap or a short meditation and let everything settle down. When you rise, you will have replenished your energy. You'll be calmer, steadier, and more grounded, connected in deeper and softer measure to that intangible source that is spirit.

As you become more integrated, and go out into the world letting more and more of your true self shine through, you'll respond differently than in your past, both to familiar circumstances and to new ones. I hope you feel safe being you, and that your new skill sets include both curiosity and a willingness to engage with people without needing to armor up. I hope you will be able to transmute any negative energy that comes towards you. To turn it into light. Have it pass through you and not get stuck. Then you'll be able to write your new story and make it happier and safer, to inhale more deeply, and share yourself with the folks who need your unique wisdom.

Take a few moments to remember the stories you used to describe yourself at the start and middle of this journey. Then pick one that you knew so well you could tell it in your sleep to people you just met, and that old friends could lip-synch word for word.

What's shifted? How do you feel about the changes?

As you go forward, choose which stories you embrace and share. You have earned that authority.

Let go of the ones that no longer serve you. And take pleasure in writing your new history and future.

STRIPES AND PLAIDS

Collage artists tell us stories through the assemblages they create. At times a small part of a piece will catch our eye, and send us down a thought stream. We're all so nuanced in our preferences that what registers as subtle to one may be too vivid for another. So I land pretty close to where I started, that what matters most is understanding your own story. Because at some point all those stories combine to create the soundtrack of humanity's bigger story. It's what the TV show *This Is Us* does to us weekly, pulling our heartstrings while we root for the good folks to thrive.

That's why people I know stand at a busy intersection weekly, holding signs to protest injustice. They get all manner of honks and fingers from drivers-by. Mostly they are witnessed, and witness themselves in their courage. Each day they stand there affirms their hope and commitment to making things different. When we look at our histories, we all see the stitched-together places and the scars we've picked up in skirmishes along the way. But others see our courage and stamina.

A few years ago, I did a backyard remodel that gave me

a patch of sunny new garden. I put in two ostensibly dwarf dahlias. Apparently they like it, because now they're tall and robust. Both were labeled Orange Ball. I imagined saffron orbs. Instead I got plants like the mis-paired Gene Wilder/ Donald Sutherland twins in *Start the Revolution Without Me*, a comedy classic. The buds look the same. But one becomes spiky yellow with fiery-red tips, while the other is white and pink, innocent and soft. They sit close, and in early summer it's hard to look at them together, until there are so many blooms that your brain registers only color and joy. It's satisfying knowing they're so exactly what they are. It's more than just making do, because I could move one or both. But I've grown to like their lack of symmetry, and watching them trick out each year into their unique and special selves. Each element tells a story, and together they tell a bigger one. For it to work, you have to allow each piece to announce itself and to make friends and family with the neighbors.

When I grew up, people were trained to wear clothes that matched. Solids with solids or solids with stripes, plaid, paisley, polka dots, or pattern, but never only two from column B. It took hippies to shake us loose. And because most of us were high, we delighted in what glittered and beguiled. Anyone who has dressed a three-year-old knows the style, but most adults grow out of it. When Ronnie and Bill took over, people reverted to the classics: making money, buying stuff, and flowing with the prevailing fashion. But we oldsters are still sorta striped and sorta plaid, maybe with some paisley or tie-dye thrown in. On any given day or decade we might seem narcissistic or philanthropic, driven or lazy, compulsive or indifferent. Our moods and interests change without any reason an observer might discern. It makes us hard to predict, and perhaps even more interesting, unless of course we're not (ugh!), in which case flee while you can, because time is too precious to spend being bored.

I used to have a nightmare about the worst people to be trapped in an elevator with: a specific relative, Nancy Reagan, and a then-colleague. This was before the *Seinfeld* finale. Both derived imagery from a Sartre play, *No Exit*. In my horror scenario the people were mean, selfish, and lacked boundaries, any of which would get them expelled from my garden.

Most of us interest ourselves, but to others we show up on a continuum from bland to threatening, or interested in completely irrelevant things. In my brief foray into online dating, (not for the faint of heart), I quickly wearied of hobbies like camping, kayaking, and RV travel, about which I cared not a whit. Where was someone like me? Oh, right, I've already got her.

What makes us interesting is our mishmash of self. The unique combos of what we love, what we avoid, and what ticks us off. Preferences in food, movies, books, and music are easy. Religions get tougher, but I don't know any saints. We're all messy mongrels, inside and out. So any one group claiming the moral high ground is both arrogant and wrong. Too many have died to impose or defend against that very belief. We are a stiff-necked species, and history, it seems, is a very poor teacher. Collective memory tilts too fast and often towards revenge; too rarely to the love-thy-neighbor side of being human.

I prefer the live-and-let-live world of diversity and disarray. A place where I can post a serene Buddha image captioned, "I'm a believer in peace and love, but I say fuck a lot." My caveat was that I'm from Philly, but I'm no less reverent for my language. I just invoke it differently than some, and would rather be playful in my cursing than righteous in my arrogance. Everyone swears a blue streak with the right provocation; I wish you few of them.

That's part of the message. Don't be so serious or judgmental. If you don't like someone else's fundamentalism, fight it by loosening up on your own. Whatever your closely held beliefs, give them an extra rinse or two in the wash. Practice loving-kindness more and judgment less. I'm not talking about abandoning your values. We're all needed on the front lines to make this world kinder, gentler, healthier, and happier. But if we could do so while respecting others, our world would get quieter and more peaceful a whole lot faster.

If I ran the world there'd be some very basic rules: No killing. No racism, sexism, or abuse. Everyone sleeps safe and warm, with a tummy that's not empty or growling. Kids get time to play, and adults to think. Weekends and Sabbaths all around. Nobody needs to be afraid. Everybody has big dreams. Art and music back into public education. Clean energy, gun reform, and reliable public transit. Investments in science and technology. Reversing climate change. The whole 99 Percent laundry list. And yes, the One Percent can pay more to make it so.

I'm an old-fashioned believer in social programs and in a world of peace, love, diversity, and harmony. It shouldn't be too much to ask. But too often that dream bumps against a greedy wardrobe of suits and power, folks dressed to subordinate others, and keep us quarreling among ourselves, when the bigger problem is that they're pulling our strings.

So how to shed our khakis and oxfords, our uniforms of power or complacency? How do we shake up our wardrobes, learn to appreciate each other in sarongs and dashikis, in day-glow yoga pants, or our comfiest jeans? We've got to lighten up and unleash the death grip of what we believe. We need to expand our worldviews a lot. The sooner the better.

Start in the simplest ways. Read a new author. Try a new vegetable. Walk in a different park. Visit some one else's sanctuary. Volunteer for a new cause. Shake up your routine so that your orbits intersect with new and different folks.

And, at least one day a week, wear something so different from your regular wardrobe that people notice. Talk and laugh and hug lots more, because a world of stripes and plaids is just a helluva lot more fun.

In Service

Sometimes I think introspection is a luxury in a world beset by trauma. But I always conclude that we all need soul wrestling. We need access to more and deeper wisdom to heal, so we can make our world safer and more nurturing for everyone.

There are folks who've never colored outside the lines between kindergarten and their Ph.D. Now, we've come up with the idea of a gap year. Time to travel, volunteer, or learn something completely unrelated to paying the rent. It creates spaciousness in personality and life choices. Yes, it's a luxury. First you need shelter, food, and safety taken care of. Refugees or the homeless are on survival's front lines, while we entitled others get to focus on cooking up a tastier life. In turn we're obligated to help as and when we can. So stop often in your happiness to think beyond the context of your life, beyond the needs of your day and the wants of your aspirations. How can you help make this place better for us all?

In autumn 2016, a spontaneous Facebook community, Pantsuit Nation, swelled to millions. There was deep sharing and support as people posted stories of their lives: vivid, painful, scary, cautionary, encouraging, and ultimately healing confessionals for the person who wrote their truth and for the readers who witnessed and honored it. Like the tell-your-darkest-secret-on-a-postcard site that went viral decades ago. The postings were cathartic and necessary for us to face the new reality we'd need to function in. We had to face our pain and fear before we could choose to kiss it goodbye and good riddance. We needed to go through that passage, raw and painful as it was, to be able to do our work.

Driving to a new coffee shop "office," I heard an NPR reporter interviewing America's then poet laureate, Juan Felipe Herrera, whose tenure had been bookended by mass shootings at a black church in Charleston and a gay bar in Orlando. They spoke about the role of poetry as a means of expression, and the idea of poetry being "in service" to language, a concept dear to my heart.

In Jodi Taylor's charming series of time-traveling historians, *The Chronicles of St. Mary's,* she vividly portrays how we're here to save one another. It's more than just witnessing. We're here to reach out an arm, to pull a friend out of the line of fire, to give someone a shove in the right direction, or whatever our assignment is in any particular karmic moment. It may be as simple as escorting someone across the street, bringing chicken soup to a sick friend, or helping a disabled neighbor. It might be as obscure as speaking what needs to be overheard by a perfect stranger. But if we're all in service, the world gets better.

There have been times I've wished for the ease of a Vulcan mind meld. The ability to take what I'm thinking and transplant it into someone else's head, and to fully receive what's in theirs. I use words and occasional arm waving to try and accomplish this, but we're never completely sure that we've been fully heard or understood. As humans, we get pretty close when we're newly infatuated, both halves straining towards the common center. We experience that togetherness after tragedies like 9/11, watching again and again in disbelief and without understanding. Sharing our sorrows and hopes for a better and more caring world, standing in the rain with our flickering candles.

The poet spoke of service as "continuous action." It reminded me of a conversation with a friend, who threatened my caution about writing this book with a promise to publish it after I was dead if I hadn't. My friend asked, "Why are you writing?" And I answered as honestly as I could, "Because this book keeps showing up. It keeps talking to me and telling me what to say." It reminded me of my goddaughter, who often said she felt the circling souls of her future children come to visit. I get it. I hope you do too.

He asked, "Does it come from service?" And I replied, "Yes." Among my deepest beliefs is that we're all here to help one another, that we're each an agent of karma, consciously or not, for the folks we encounter. For the people who know they need us and ask for help, and even for the ones who resent our very presence. Our fates intersect for a reason; the lessons are ripe and present and meant for us both.

We're here to push, to help, to goad, and to remind, to listen and bear witness. To make one another laugh and cry and remember our common humanity. I translate that as servicing our common goal of becoming the best humans we can be.

That means helping us teach and learn with greater compassion, which makes learning our lessons more bearable. It also helps us learn our lessons more quickly, and, with luck, less painfully. That's true for all our lessons, be they big or small, quick or persistent. If we're lucky and paying good enough attention to hear them, allies appear who nudge us towards higher consciousness. If we're not, we get sent different teachers; with them our lessons might take much longer, maybe even lots longer than we'll remember being this us.

I believe in language as a vehicle. In the utility of words to communicate thought and feeling, to be evocative as well as instructive. I think language can open us and challenge us. It can make us more receptive to figuring out the answers to whatever karmic homework we're wrestling with at the time.

Writing this book has been a deep and expansive process for me. Everything you have done I have done too. Sometimes my writing started as journaling and became the seed of a chapter. Sometimes writing about an idea led me to hidden chambers of my heart. I no longer distinguish as strictly as I may once have done between mind, body, and spirit. It's all about integration, and letting our fullest and truest self speak. It's about being in service in the world. So whether my writing voice comes through as Your Jewish Fairy Godmother, as Reb Helen, or as messy me wrestling with my private demons, it's almost always about wanting a better world for us all.

Among my favorite writers is Salman Rushdie, whose command of language is occasionally staggering. His earliest novel is a garden of puns, a morass in which characters swim and sometimes drown. It's an awkward book, a romp of quantum physics, ancient fables, and the quest for self-knowing. Rushdie would enjoy making every pun on the word *service*, from the hotly sexual to the saintly aspirations of the godly.

At its Latin root, *service* ties to bondage; but it has evolved to mean a source of helpful supply, even kindness.

I'm rarely shy with a lowbrow joke, but I'm eternally striving for goodness. Irreverent as it may sometimes be, I hope my language is always in the service of our highest good, in the hope that our hearts will open and our souls expand and that we'll find at least a little of the truth and goodness that we seek. I have hope that our inner light will shine through just a wee bit more, and that each day will make us lighter and wiser and more able and willing to serve others as well as ourselves.

Writing is ultimately how I'm most in service. As I edited this book for the last time, I did the Ten Commandments exercise again. Here's what showed up as my set of intentions for the next phase of my life: *Be happy and grounded. Find the joy in every choice. Let clarity and integrity guide you. Trust your knowing. Let the words and light shine through. Stay open. Listen, listen, listen. Connect from the heart. Love deeply. Stay in service.*

You can decide how best you can be of service. I hope you do, because the rest of us need you doing what you do.

Remember that holy spark we talked about way back when? In Kabbalah each of those sparks—in you, in me, in each of us and every living thing—came from the birth of the universe, when all the Oneness was dispersed. Our responsibility as humans is to reunite those sparks. In Judaism that is called "tikkum olam," which means, "the healing of the world." I believe that healing begins within each of us, and that we have a responsibility to everyone else to share our goodness until the world is holier and more whole. I hope our journey has helped.

Some final questions:

Are you happier than when you began this book?

How do you answer the "What do you really want?" question today?

Would that include helping others become happier too? How will you do that?

Say Good Night, Gracie

Last century, when I was young, I watched a show starring George Burns and Gracie Allen. It was an anachronism even in its day: an upper class, married pair, over-dressed and dealing with social situations of a former age. You might remember Burns from *Oh, God!* as a short, raspy, cigar-smoking voice of authority. Gracie was the Edith Bunker role model: ditzy, high-pitched, erratic, and unpredictable, but surprisingly wise. Each show ended with her nattering on about something. Burns would take a big puff of his cigar and say, "Say good night, Gracie." In her final goodbye, Gracie would say something so useful or funny that you wanted them never to leave.

When I studied various spiritual lineages, I looked for their version of crazy wisdom, like the folks on the *narrenschiff*: holy fools who tell you what you most need to know, exactly when and how you most need to know it, even if it's delivered as a riddle that takes time to decipher. It happens when the song in your earbuds blurts the advice you've been waiting to hear, or a Facebook post or a fortune cookie gives you exactly the succinct insight that endless conversations with your friends or therapist have failed to generate. If you're lucky, that's how the universe works. It serves up what you most need to hear right on time and gets you back on track.

What I believe above all, what I count on daily, and what has been shown true more often than I can remember is this: the wisdom you need will come to you. It will be delivered as a gift, to honor that you've shown up and are doing your work. It will come when you might least expect, perhaps even after you've abandoned all but the last shred of hope. It will come in forms that you cannot demand or conjure, though you should ask for answers often and clearly, and keep warm and welcoming landing zones in your heart and psyche.

You need to keep your channels open. You need to be receptive and listening. Because everything you need is within you and accessible to you, just waiting for you to perceive it.

Pay attention. Wrestle time from your days to stay open. Live with as much awareness as you can. Consciousness is remembering answers that are just a nanosecond from your knowing. If that's your compass, you can get to wherever you want to go.

There's a core belief in Judaism to choose life. I would add, choose joy. Everything you want or need is here. It welcomes and nourishes you.

Why would you choose anything else?

COME FULL CIRCLE/BENEDICTION

We made the trek. At times the journey wasn't as hard as we had feared. Other times it was worse. But the edges of pain will dull with time, and the sweetness of victory will remain. The messy places we used to despair about, we no longer fear. We invite them to visit, make them comfy, and laugh about old times. Enjoy a glass or two; toast how we have become new. Then sleep the sleep of the righteous because it's mostly, mostly true.

We're lighter and happier in our souls than were at the start. I hope that's true for you.

When I'm making real progress, things happen easily and simply. There's no resistance. Just energy and a quickening sense that I'm on track. I hope you feel that more often than you did. Remember to say thanks when you do.

I hope you're happier and kinder. That your troubles are few and your curiosity great. And that part of your life is for the sheer joy of living, however you experience that, whether it's art or sport or sitting in your garden, talking to whomever you wish and dreaming in whatever your heart language has become.

I hope the heavy places feel lighter and clearer. That your ability to forgive is swifter and softer.

I hope your path is easy. And that the next time you begin this journey, for there will be so many more chances, that it is simpler. That the answers you need come faster and more clearly.

There's a ceremony in Judaism called The Priestly Blessing. I offer the spirit, not the letter, of the prayer:

> *May you be held in the center of all that is eternal.*
> *May you be filled with light and feel blessed.*
> *May you always find peace.*

Whatever makes you feel that way, go do lots more of it, for as long as it does. Then find another and another after that. Be sure-footed and safe on your journey. Be joyous, and filled with awe and wonder.

Then please share all that with all the rest of us.

ACKNOWLEDGMENTS

Thanks to all my loving friends who helped me during this journey. They know my heart and soul, and each contributed in so many and beautiful ways to making this book what it has become.

Thanks to my book doulas for their expertise and guidance: Allison Tivnon and Jen Weaver-Neist for developmental perspective; Vinnie Kinsella for design; Robyn Crummer-Olson and Stephanie Anderson for strategic planning; HannahRose Rand for insulating me from technology; and Holly Andres for a fun photo shoot.

Thanks to my soul sisters who read all my drafts, and cheered me on, lifting me up and kicking my butt as the moment required: Sydney Ashland, Devorah Henderson, Flaxen Conway, and Stella Griffith. And to Luke Adler for being my soul brother and needling me to begin.

Thanks to my draft readers, proof readers, and smart, sharp-eyed friends, who offered insightful comments and helpful corrections large and small: Ellen Rifkin, Beth Rankin, Julie Cresswell, Myrna Hant, Carolena Nerricio, Morgan Hunt, Marjorie Feldman, Leah Riordan, and others who read imperfect drafts and made suggestions. Any remaining mistakes are entirely my own.

Thanks to my essence friends, who listened to my fears and dreams and loved me none the less: Mara Wile, Wendy Jones-Epstein, Johanna Mitchell, Eileen Traylor, Bette Phelan, Judy Jurgaitis, Luba Jillings, Deborah Brady, and Sam Kimelblot. Each said what I needed to hear when it mattered most. I hope you recognize pieces of yourself in these pages.

A quote from David Mitchell that became both truth and challenge, as did the family of foxes that came to live in my yard as I wrote the first solid draft: If you show someone something you've written, you give them a sharpened stake, lie down in your coffin, and say, 'When you're ready.' Both taught me new lessons about openness, trust, and joy.

Thanks to all for helping me say *Yes*.

PERMISSIONS

Rumi, from *The Glance: Songs Of Soul-Meeting*, translated by Coleman Barks, translation copyright © 1999 by Coleman Barks. Used by permission of Viking Books, an imprint of Penguin Publishing Group, a division of Penguin Random House LLC. All rights reserved.

From *State of Wonder* by Barbara Kingsolver, Copyright © 2002 by Barbara Kingsolver. Reprinted by permission of Harper Collins Publishers.

Brene Brown, TED talk January, 2011, reprinted by permission of Brene Brown Media Team

Yann Martel, from *Life of Pi,* Copyright © 2001, Harcourt, reprinted by permission of the author

Rumi, from *Fragments, Ecstasies*, translation by Daniel Liebert, Copyright © 1981 reprinted by permission of Sunstone Press

Natalie Goldberg, from *Writing Down the Bones*, Copyright © 1986, reprinted by permission of Shambhala Publications

From *State of Wonder* by Anne Patchett, Copyright © 2011 by Anne Patchett. Reprinted by permission of Harper Collins Publishers

Pema Chodren, from *Start Where You Are*: *A Guide for*

ABOUT THE AUTHOR

Helen Rosenau is a New Age soul with Old World wisdom. A blend of East Coast savvy and West Coast mellow. She knows what hurts when it's been stretched too far. She's been around long enough to collect some thumps and learned how to bounce. She loves the cosmic joyrides of love, creativity, and exploring the cosmos. To know what matters to her, what she thinks about, and what she makes, visit yourjewishfairygodmother.com and kabbalahglass.com. Those sites, this book, and an evening sipping and talking by the fire would give you a good feeling for who she has been, is now, and wants to become.

CPSIA information can be obtained
at www.ICGtesting.com
Printed in the USA
LVHW081712120319
610370LV00014B/672/P

9 781732 533752